Waldorf Schools

Volume I

Waldorf Schools

Volume I

Kindergarten and Early Grades

Thirty-three articles from "Education as an Art",
Bulletin of the Waldorf Schools of North America
1940 - 1978

Selected and edited by Ruth Pusch,
with an introduction
by Betty Staley

MERCURY PRESS
Spring Valley, New York
1993

Copyright © 1993 by Mercury Press

ISBN 0-929979-29-X

Published in the USA by:

MERCURY PRESS
Fellowship Community
241 Hungry Hollow Road
Spring Valley, NY 10977

Contents

I. IDEAS AND INSIGHTS

II. THE WALDORF KINDERGARTEN

III. THE FIRST FIVE GRADES

IV. THE WHOLE SCHOOL

Introduction

For over seventy years Waldorf education has been educating children all over the world. In the United States the Waldorf school movement has gradually and inconspicuously gathered strength and depth. The graduates of the schools have gone into the "real world" and instead of feeling they had been educated in a "different", even perhaps "strange" educational system, they are finding they have a reservoir of strength, understanding, and vision which they can offer to their classmates in college, to their colleagues at work, and in their personal lives. This affirmation is experienced on many levels of life—being a parent of a young child among a group of mothers, being a lawyer dealing with ethical issues, working in human resources, serving patients in a medical field, being a practicing artist, and the list goes on and on.

But Waldorf education is not cloistered any longer. In the despair over education in America, educators, parents, and children are calling out for something different. Practices are being developed that parallel some of the Waldorf methods and principles. Parents are calling for Waldorf classrooms within the public schools. More and more, Waldorf educators are addressing public forums of teachers and parents. And we are being listened to. In fact, much as Rudolf Steiner indicated, Waldorf education is the education for this epoch of history. More and more we will see public school teachers dipping into Waldorf education for answers. More public workshops will be demanded. In addition, Waldorf schools continue to be born in community after community.

One of the great strengths of the Waldorf educational movement is the freedom of the teachers to create within the curricular and pedagogical guidelines. When a teacher penetrates his or her work with insights based on the anthroposophical understanding of the child, the creative wellspring is tapped, and original ways of teaching emerge.

1

It is a joy to visit Waldorf classrooms and see the many ways teachers interpret the methods and curriculum.

From 1940 through 1978 teachers have shared their experiences through the Rudolf Steiner School's bulletin entitled Education As an Art. These bulletins are a treasure trove for teachers. I have a shelf of them in my library, and many times I have pored through them looking for an article on a particular main lesson block I was preparing to teach. But how many people are as fortunate as I to have these dog-eared copies from thirty years ago?

It is a gift to Waldorf as well as public school teachers that these articles have been gathered and published in this and a second volume.

Opening the pages of this book is like having a rich and inspiring Waldorf conference in your living room. You can ponder the thoughts of a teacher who has had a particularly enlightening experience with nature stories or teaching writing or science. You can find answers to questions parents ask at parent meetings. There are rich resources here for public relations work for your school. Most of all, it presents an opportunity to meet teachers who have served the Waldorf movement over thirty years during its seedtime on this continent.

Betty Staley

I

IDEAS AND INSIGHTS

Out of the gravity of our time
There must be born
Courage for deeds.
Give to your teaching
What the spirit has given you,
And you will liberate mankind
From the nightmare
That weighs upon it
Through materialism.

Rudolf Steiner

(Translated from *Wahrspruchworte, Richtspruchworte, Sprüche und
Widmungen*. Rudolf Steiner Nachlassverwaltung, 1953)

What Do We Mean By Education as an Art?

Modern education is based upon scientific thinking, experimental in principle. The behavior of the human beings who are to be educated is studied, analyzed, compared with that of others, and certain behavior patterns are discovered. Then certain methods of teaching are applied and certain results are achieved. Since new ideas are always popping up, and since the possibilities are unlimited, there is an unending atmosphere of business and importance. The modern educator goes about his task with the same sincere determination with which the scientist goes about working out a new mechanism.

The education based upon spiritual science, however, recognizes the human being as a spiritual entity. To the teacher the child is not a complex mechanism with intricate reflexes but a divine creation.

The child is a creation who if neglected will not survive, a creation whose physical manifestation is but a vessel for his soul and spirit. Just as a fine work of art is the creation of a human being, a child is the creation of divine forces, of the spiritual world. A work of art can be compared to a child in so far as it is a creation out of the human spirit. A machine is a creation out of the pure human intellect.

The child, therefore, can be considered as a work of art with the world spirit as its creator. As teachers or parents we are destined, or one might say we are privileged, to be the world-creator's lowly servants.

If it is true therefore that the child is a work of art in the process of being created, education can only be an art and never merely a science. The painter at work at his painting submerges or lives with his entire being in his creation and thus finds harmony and balance of forms and colors; and thus the teacher must live with his entire being in God's creation, if he is to be an artist rather than a scientist.

(1951)   —William Harrer

4

The First Waldorf School

On a hillside overlooking the city of Stuttgart in the valley of the Neckar there was enacted on March 30, 1938, a scene of great impressiveness which, taken together with its sequel seven years later and its predecessor in 1919, forms a tableau of three scenes of great importance for education in Germany and throughout the world.

These three scenes in the life of the Free Waldorf School are dramatic examples of the triumph of man's spirit over adversity and the willingness of people to suffer for the sake of an educational ideal.

The Closing under Hitler

On this spring day of 1938 the Waldorf School, one of the last free institutions under National Socialism, was being closed by government order and the final assembly was made the occasion of a pilgrimage by friends of the school who had cherished and supported it through the dark days and had now come to join with the students and teachers in a pledge of renewal some day and by some means.

The great hall of the school on the hill was packed. At the front near the stage were the small children swirling about their teachers like tiny wavelets lapping at an island. Behind sat the older classes, each with its teacher; and the young people of the upper grades closed the ranks.

The rows at the back were filled with grown-ups, men and women from many walks of life, parents of present and former pupils, students from the Waldorf Training College and the friends who had come from afar. From the balconies hundreds of former pupils looked down, once more at home for a brief moment in the school they had loved.

Everyone present, even the smallest children who had no understanding of the workings of the political tragedy in which their lives had been caught up, knew what this last assembly meant. How different from the other joyous occasions when they had gathered here!

The ceremony was simple and direct. Each teacher spoke to his or her class, and through his words each child received the message that his beloved school was no more. Then the school orchestra played the Fifth Symphony of Beethoven, which one of the school's founders had called the Symphony of Destiny. Finally, Count Fritz Bothmer, the school's chairman who had conducted the long and painful negotiations with the Nazi authorities, rose.

The building in which they were assembled, Count Bothmer said, had been constructed on the form of a cross and from the spot where he stood, at the junction of the two arms, the founders of the Waldorf School had often spoken to parents and pupils.

"Here," he said, "our most beautiful and impressive festivals have taken place. Here the heart of the Waldorf School has shone forth most luminously. This institution is founded on the form of the cross and upon the name of Him who died upon the cross but continues to live in those human beings who offer Him a dwelling place in their hearts. Therefore, the heart of this school also continues to live."

At this point Count Bothmer asked the assembly to rise, and continued: "I have now the task of pronouncing that, upon the decree of the Wuerttemberg government, the Waldorf School is closed. Let us then, with the power of love, seal up our school in the deepest recesses of our hearts for the future."

On the following day nearly all the thousand and more present at this ceremony were present at another scene as far removed as is possible to imagine. This one was enacted at the Stuttgart railway station where Adolf Hitler, returning in triumph from the accomplishment of the Anschluss in Austria, stopped off to receive the frenzied *Heils* of his followers and the homage-by-order of all the others.

Teachers, pupils and friends of the now defunct Waldorf School stood on the fringes of the hysterical crowd, unable to see into the future for themselves or for Germany, unable even to think beyond the day, but knowing in their hearts that the day would come, however long delayed, when dictators were not and education would be free again.

Rebuilding out of the Ruins

That day came for the Waldorf School in October of 1945 in vastly different physical and spiritual surroundings on the same hillside, when the school was reopened under what difficulties never will be adequately told. But here was living proof that the words spoken and the pledge taken in 1938 had not been forgotten.

The once lovely city lay in ruins. Its streets were littered with rubble and the houses were burnt-out shells. People lived in cellars and provisional shelters. The children of the town, grown up without fathers, presented a pitiful picture as, ragged, barefoot and hungry, full of restlessness and fear and weakened moral feeling, they played among the twisted beams and piles of rubbish or gathered cigarette ends on the pavement to sell at black market prices.

But there on a fragment of the wall of the wrecked main building of the Waldorf School, painted in large letters by some former student, were the words, "We Will Be Back." These words had stood for seven years against both the vindictiveness of the Nazi Gestapo and the fury of Allied bombings, and still were there as a symbol that the spirit of freedom had not died.

And so, on the very day the occupation troops entered Stuttgart, a little group of people emerged from the chaos to meet in a suburban house and discuss the fate of the children. Some were former teachers at the Waldorf School, some were parents and some, former pupils now grown to manhood and womanhood in a time of destruction when all that remained seemed to be an animal-like need to struggle for survival. All had carried the school in their hearts through seven years of hardship.

This group was addressed by Dr. Erich Schwebsch, a former teacher of the school, who told them that the words spoken in 1938 had not been mere phrases and that now was the time to start again even though the difficulties might seem insurmountable. The need to reopen, Dr. Schwebsch said, was urgent, for the hope of Germany lay with these children who roamed the rubble and knew not where to turn.

The school had been bombed out, its main building was a burned-out ruin and all other buildings were badly damaged. The school yard was a huge mass of wreckage that only the most modern salvage machines seemed likely to clear. But into this mess of destruction Dr. Schwebsch and his band plunged with hardly more than their hands as tools.

As they worked, their numbers grew. At the original meeting several former pupils, now grown beyond school age, volunteered to bring the word to teachers and friends wherever they could be found. On bicycles they crossed zone lines, searching everywhere, and one by one those teachers who had survived came trickling back.

All that long first summer they worked, on the edge of starvation, and the trickle of those in whom the spirit had been kept alive grew into a stream. They came from wherever they were and by whatever means of travel they could find as soon as the word had been brought to them.

In that summer the rubble was cleared with a few spades and many pairs of hands. The damage to minor buildings was repaired and two provisional wooden structures were built. In a time when no building material was apparently to be had, these people somehow found it. Their own homes were in ruins but the school came first. They acquired the material actually by a complicated system of barter and exchange in which food, cigarettes and clothing were more valuable than gold. And they had enormous help from the friendly American military authorities.

In October, 1945, the school re-opened with a solemn and touching ceremony that stemmed directly from the closing ceremony of 1938. More than 500 pupils were present on opening day, twelve complete grades were formed, and of these only a handful in the two upper classes had been pupils seven years earlier.

The difficulties these children and their parents had to overcome in order to attend classes were almost incredible. No family had enough to eat or enough clothes to go around. Some pupils could come only irregularly because the family had only one pair of shoes that was shared. Transportation was so poor that some children from the surrounding country had to leave home at dawn each day and did not get back until long after dark.

Still they came, and from the first day the school had a long waiting list of families eager for their children to attend.

While the rest of the city and the rest of Germany bemoaned their fate, the Waldorf teachers, pupils and parents began their work, full of faith in the future. An army officer present at the opening said that the school was "like an island of hope in an ocean of despair." Dr. Schwebsch spoke of the "blessing of a second start."

Founding and Growth—"A Lasting Human Purpose"

To understand what had taken place here on the hillside, it is necessary now to turn to the opening scene of the tableau which was enacted at a time of almost similar chaos in Germany. In 1919 the world had blundered into a peace that was a continuation of war, and the ideas with which men hoped to build a new and better world could not cope with the realities of life.

The thunderstorm of the First World War has not taught men that the outworn conceptions of the 18th and 19th centuries could no longer apply, for men had slept through the storm, emerging from it with the same basic habits of thought with which they entered.

There were men in 1919, however, who recognized the true situation and who saw that the ideas with which it was hoped to build a permanent peace were hopelessly outdated and could produce only confusion. Because of the break-down of outer conditions, Germany was open to new impulses as she had never been before, and in the midst of these conditions a farsighted industrialist, Dr. Emil Molt, owner of the Waldorf Astoria cigarette factory in Stuttgart, came to Rudolf Steiner, philosopher and educator, with the request that he found a school for the children of Molt's 4,250 factory workers.

Emil Molt was a man of wealth and great influence, and he was deeply concerned with the social and economic problems of the times. He recognized that all these problems had their source in the central problem of the human being himself; he wished, in a time of economic breakdown and social revolution, to use his wealth for a lasting human purpose.

He believed that the most effective way to achieve this was to found a school where children would receive a truly human education which would help them to take their places in life no matter what the outer conditions might be. And he turned to Rudolf Steiner as the educator whom he considered best able to create such a school.

Steiner accepted the task on two conditions: that he be free from every political, economic or religious control in following his educational principles, and that children of every social and economic class be admitted. The school was to be "free," he said, as an artist is free to create out of the necessities of his material.

Curriculum and teaching methods were to evolve from insight into the nature of man, arrived at by means of the investigation of supersensible realities according to the disciplines of scientific thought and observation. It was to the winning of this knowledge and the development of a clear, contemporary path to its achievement that Rudolf Steiner had devoted his life and it was the recognition by Emil Molt that his knowledge awakened creative capacities in those who worked with it, leading them to practical and helpful results, which had moved him to approach Rudolf Steiner on behalf of the school he wished to found. This was not to be just one more pedagogical experiment, but a response to the spiritual and social needs of the times.

The faculty would be the real leaders of the school and, under no outside influence, would be free to build the school out of its own necessity. The school was to be maintained entirely by gift money if that were possible, or by gift money and tuitions if it were not. The ideal would be no tuition fees at all, but this proved impossible because of an already impending terrible inflation in Germany.

This educational idea was in complete contrast to the system then prevailing in Germany, where the *Abitur*, the stiff entrance examination for the universities, was the goal of secondary education. German children went to elementary public schools where tuition was free, from the ages of six to ten. Then the parents decided, chiefly according to the state of their purses, whether the child should go to the Gymnasium for eight more years and become an "intellectual," or stay in the Volksschule and prepare for a manual profession. The child's future was thus determined at the age of ten and the tradition of the German education was to create separate social castes.

Dr. Molt purchased for the new school a building that had housed a fashionable restaurant, bringing down upon himself at the start the disapproval of the elite of Stuttgart who had dined there for generations. Here, Steiner gathered together the handful of men and women he had selected as teachers and conducted an intensive course in the new pedagogy with daily lectures, seminars and demonstrations.

On the day the Waldorf School was scheduled to open, nearly 400 children with their future teachers gathered in the courtyard of the former restaurant building and were separated into age groups. And there, on the spot, Steiner assigned the teachers to the grades, declaring that it was necessary to see the teachers in the presence of the children before deciding which should take which group.

11

The school started under the best of auspices, with a ceremony in a large hall in the center of Stuttgart that followed immediately on this initial assembly. The hall was filled to overflowing with more than 2,000 persons, among them the Minister of Education for Wuerttemberg, a Socialist who was favorably disposed toward the new venture.

Within a year of its founding the school had about 800 pupils and at its peak about 1,000; it was limited only by its physical capacities. These pupils included boys and girls of every creed and class and from almost every part of the world. The curriculum and teaching methods attracted educators from many countries who carried them back to their own homes, with the result that schools working with the Waldorf pedagogy grew up in Switzerland, Austria, Holland, Norway, Sweden, England and the United States.

Those who knew the school at this time felt that here was a group, although still small, of young people who could break through national barriers and conventional, routine thinking to a genuine internationalism which would not be satisfied with empty phrases.

And then came 1933 and the rise of Hitler to power. From that day the Waldorf School and the, by now, nine other Steiner Schools in Germany were doomed. By their very nature they could not conform to the Nazi ideas of educations.

The reasons were bluntly stated in the press of the day. The Waldorf Schools developed individuals, whereas the task of education in a National Socialist State was to produce National Socialists. Two such opposed systems of education could not exist in a single state.

But ideas and ideals such as these live all the more intensively and inwardly when outwardly suppressed and, as the third scene in the tableau demonstrated, wherever the spirit lived in Germany unseen through the dark years, there was an ally for the cause of freedom.

At a time when the free world is struggling to unite and to find the strength to maintain its freedom, we need to strengthen the roots of freedom in the judgment and the heart of each individual citizen. The work of the Waldorf schools, wherever they may be, is a step in this direction.

(1958)   Al Laney

Independent Teachers and Independent Schools

Each of us in education today has, at one time or another, probably asked himself: if I had the chance to bring about a single change in the school system, what would it be? What might reach deep enough to make a difference from the ground up? There are perhaps several answers, but there is one of which I am very sure: place the conduct of the schools in the hands of their teachers!

There are, of course, immediately, dozens of objections.

Where will you find teachers willing to assume responsibility of this kind? How will they get administrative training? Can they command the respect of parents and community?

To which can be answered: any teacher worth his salt is willing to assume responsibility; he will learn as he acts and will seek the required training, and will certainly command respect to the degree that he proves himself able to manage his own professional affairs.

This is not said theoretically but out of the experience of many years as a teacher and administrator of a faculty-run school. What distinguishes such a school? How does it work?

There is no prescribed formula according to which a faculty-run school operates. Each school is individual; its circumstances differ and so do the personalities involved. In one situation, administration may be at a minimum, leadership may rotate rapidly, the classroom teacher may deal directly and almost single-handedly with parents, everything is relaxed and informal. Another situation may call for far more structure and permanence. But one thing is essential if the school is to be genuinely faculty-run: there must be no doubt as to who is, in fact, responsible and there must be confidence that sooner or later every question which fundamentally affects the policy of the school will come to the faculty for discussion and that decisions made in this group will have the full support of the school.

Here there would seem to be no choice of means. Unless a faculty meets regularly and there is full and frank discussion, unless decisions are made and these decisions are made to stick, there may be lip service to the ideal but in reality the authority lies elsewhere. The faculty meeting is, indeed, the heart of the enterprise. This is where judgment is formed and leadership emerges. Here confidence is slowly created out of a common striving and out of a responsibility which is shared. All this takes time and is not easy, for a genuine faculty is not just a random union of its teachers—with their individual gifts and capacities—but a self-directing and living organism, distinct and wiser than the sum of its parts. It is not a democracy in which each opinion receives equal weight but a true republic in which each personality is accorded respect and freedom and in which there is confidence and the courage to support individual initiative and excellence. From such a center everything else flows.

Who, then, constitutes the faculty? Is every teacher automatically included? Is it a limited, inner circle who have worked together for many years? To this there will almost certainly be different answers. In order to become specific allow me to describe the way in which things have evolved in a particular school, the Rudolf Steiner School, New York.

Responsibility rests primarily with a body known as the Faculty Council in the New York school. A teacher becomes eligible once he has been with the school for at least a year and has expressed the wish to remain on a permanent basis. Upon the invitation of the Faculty Council he is asked to meet with it, participating fully in all discussions, but withholding a final voice in the decisions. After a year's experience both parties reconsider and, if the original decision is mutually confirmed, the teacher becomes a permanent council member.

Membership in the Faculty Council also makes one a member of the Rudolf Steiner School Inc., the legal entity which owns the school. Organized as a membership corporation under the laws of the State of New York for the purpose of conducting a non-profit educational institution, the corporation includes the Faculty Council and other individuals who may be invited to join. The individual members are drawn from the ranks of parents, former parents and friends who have demonstrated their permanent interest and their ability to help the school without wishing to dominate and control. The corporation elects its Board of Directors which includes teachers and non-Faculty Council members and which concerns itself with legal and financial questions in close cooperation with the faculty leadership of the school.

Authority is delegated by the Faculty Council to individuals and to groups who then become responsible for the daily administration of the school. A Faculty Chairman is elected annually with no fixed term and is re-elected as often as need be. He performs the functions of a principal or headmaster but with the active support of the entire faculty as his authority, not the appointment by an outside board. An Executive and a Finance Committee, selected by the Chairman and confirmed by the Faculty Council, assist in the conduct of administrative affairs. As the school grew and administration became more complex and time-consuming, the need for independent pedagogical leadership within the faculty made itself felt and led to the selection of a teacher as a coordinator and chairman of pedagogical affairs. Several teachers share with him the task of preparing the bi-weekly meetings, attended by every member of the teaching staff, in which class reports are made and discussed, individual children are presented, questions of curriculum and method

15

brought forward and recommendations proposed. Responsibility for faculty study programs, teacher training, parent study groups, etc., also fall within the scope of the pedagogical leadership.

The present administrative arrangements at the Rudolf Steiner School which, on the whole, serve the school very well indeed, did not spring into existence full-blown like Athena from the head of Zeus. They have changed and developed over the years. The school was founded nearly forty years ago by a group of devoted teachers and persons interested in Rudolf Steiner education who were, as characterized by an early friend, endowed with "enthusiasm unhampered by experience"! In these first years the faculty's zeal and inexperience was guided and protected—sometimes perhaps also obstructed and interfered with—by a governing board of trustees in which teachers were not included. Changes of school personnel were frequent, money was short, the parent body fluctuated, in every direction there seemed a great deal to be learned, but there was also an idealism and a pioneer enthusiasm difficult ever to match again. There were long years of small numbers, combined classes and great sacrifice. At an especially discouraging period the board of directors concluded: we have done what we could with the knowledge and experience which we bring to the school's problems from our various backgrounds in life and this has not been enough. We are not sure of the school's future; we are not sure where it is headed nor what needs to be done. It is the teachers who carry the school through their work, their capacities, and their willingness to accept salaries which are less than they would earn elsewhere, and it is the teachers who believe in the school and know what they think should be done. Let us draw the logical conclusion and hand over the responsibility for the school to those on whose shoulders the actuality rests. This was done. The board of directors resigned as a body and a new organization evolved, which was later formally described in legal language in the new constitution of the school.

This evolution, as a result of which practical administration, including finance and legal ownership, was placed in the hands of those who already carried the spiritual and moral initiative and educational responsibility, proved to be a turning point in the school's history. From this time forward the school moved ahead; it grew and prospered. This is not to imply that the transition to faculty responsibility was the sole factor in the school's development, but it released creative energies, freed initiative and gave the school a clear direction which called forth confidence and a practical response.

What proved a decisive blessing for a relatively small private school in New York City has also far wider implications. There appears no doubt that one of the underlying motives behind the recent New York City teachers' strike is the revolt of the teacher against the dead weight of bureaucratic routine, the urge for direct participation in shaping the program for which, in the end, the classroom teacher is expected to be responsible. Campus unrest from coast to coast is, in part, a protest against the anonymous teacher, the research- and committee-man, the individual who stands with only a fraction of himself before his students and engages but a small part of their humanity in the learning exchange. The teacher, however, who is not merely an employee but has a personal stake in the institution, who is co-responsible to meet the problems with which life confronts a school or college today is far more actively engaged and stands, therefore, with a different conviction in the educational process.

Beyond everything else in life today we need creative human personalities; personalities with access to a source of insight which can lend support to their human judgment and their moral initiative—insight which is a source of strength, yet which leaves one free. This is, in the end, a question of individual self-development, a challenge to each of us to

17

become spiritually alive. This will, I believe, eventually come to be recognized as Rudolf Steiner's outstanding contribution to the spiritual life of our time: that he pioneered the way by which each individual can awaken the spiritual capacities which slumber in his own soul and which can lead him along a conscious, self-disciplined path to the spirit which underlies the world in all its outer aspects. This is the path along which a teacher becomes creative; this is the intangible link between the teacher and the child. This is something which can not be regulated, can not be compelled, but which can only come about in freedom. This is the deeper reason why a teacher must be free.

The freedom of the individual teacher to teach according to his conscience and to participate in the running of his school is, however, not the starting point but the consequence of another, more comprehensive and basic condition: the independence of cultural-spiritual life within the body social. Until the sciences and the arts, until education above all, have achieved their independence from political and from economic control there will be no ground for lesser freedoms. By suggesting that the schools should be placed in the hands of their teachers one is also saying: find the way to set the spirit free in every branch of its activity—give the artist, the researcher, the philosopher, the physician, the creative statesman, the business originator, the teacher, the man of religion, give to each the element without which he is only a fraction of his potential productive self: his independence as a productive worker in the cultural sphere.

We began this article with a proposal: to call on the creative capacities of the nation's teachers by inviting them to share in the practical responsibility for managing our schools. This is no hypothetical consideration; it is being successfully done. Behind it lies a broader proposition: to recognize the fact that without freedom the spirit cannot be active anywhere. If the existence of the Rudolf Steiner schools can contribute to a practical awakening in this sphere, they will be fulfilling an important part of their original, creative pilot function.

(1967)   Henry Barnes
          (Former Chairman of the Faculty, Rudolf Steiner School)

"In our teachers' meetings, which are the heart of the whole school life, the single individualities of the children are carefully discussed, and what the teachers themselves learn from the meetings, week by week, is derived first and foremost from the consideration of the children's individualities. This is the way the teachers may perfect themselves. A child presents a whole series of riddles; out of the solving of these riddles there will develop the feelings that the teacher must carry into the class."

Rudolf Steiner
Kingdom of Childhood,
Lecture 4.

Too Much Like Work?

The worst enemy mankind ever had was the dastard who persuaded it that work, which might be the dearest joy we have, was . . . well, . . . work. As a result of that crime, almost the whole population of the world rises up o' mornings groaning like slaves at the prospect of a day of work ahead.

A debasing state of affairs, and we should not put up with it another minute! But what can be done to root out this evil that has eaten so long and deeply into men's souls?

It was claimed above that "*almost* the whole population" groans. Who are the exceptions? What makes them such? Perhaps there is a clue here that could guide everyone to freedom from his sour slavery.

The exceptions are children and the craftsman-artist. To these, each new day, far from being shadowed by depression, holds out the promise of fulfillment; their only worry is whether it will be long enough to accomplish all they have in mind to do. They live in the light of a vision so dynamic that it can literally lift them out of bed. Their hearts tingle with warmth towards their projects. So they set to work with a will sparked, as all free activity must be, by an idea, a mental image enriched and made rainbow-colorful by caring.

Let us watch them at work. Are they taking the easy way out, or quickly growing tired or cold or hungry? Not a bit of it! These little boys who have been dragging boards up a ladder all morning long to build a tree house, hammering their thumbs black and blue as they nailed them, growl with frustration when summoned in to lunch. Smaller ones nearby, wet to the gills, are assiduously draining puddles in the driveway. A homesteader slogs out through February snows to prune his orchard, aglow with dreams of trees, open to the light, hanging red and gold with fruit in autumn. The home-loving housewife scrubs up her kitchen, rejoicing in the emerging godly order. Someone else is tenderly carrying the care of a beloved invalid without feeling it a burden. A cabinet-maker puts the final polish on a piece of furniture while, above, his small daughter rearranges her doll-house, admonishes its occupants and irons their clothes with a miniscule iron. There a writer paces up and down sweating out a search for the exactly right word or phrase or picture. An instrumentalist runs over and over a passage, his attention sharpening with each repeat. An athlete drives himself mercilessly to achieve better form, greater endurance.

Are these various laborers finding their efforts "too much like work"? No, they are glorying in their activity. It is, they feel each moment, "what they came for."

Is there anything more to be desired than this?

Yet we see little children, who start out loving work, being taught to hate it. And where does this first happen? Usually in the schoolroom! That is where the slavery is bred that so few escape. In a universe where all life is in movement, where every fact seen in perspective is totally engaging, we impose stillness on lively young bodies, distort reality to dullness, make action drudgery. Those who submit—as the majority does—are conditioned to a life lived without their human birthright: work done with the joy and creativity of love.

But what are schools for if not to make children fall so deeply in love with the world that they really want to learn about it? That is the true business of schools. And if they succeed in it, all other desirable developments follow of themselves.

In a proper school, no fact would ever be presented as a soulless one, for the simple reason that there is no such thing. Every facet of reality, discovered where it lives, startles with its wonder, beauty, meaning. It is the great strength of Rudolf Steiner schools that they know and do this. So, for example, where in other schools little scholars slavishly copy the skeletal figures known as the alphabet, Steiner school beginners first hear and then paint and act out a fairy tale about each letter that reveals the enchanting life hidden in both sound and symbol. "S" may be a serpent sinuous and subtle, "W" a wave, "M" the magic mountain into which "P" the Pied Piper vanishes. Those bugbears of childhood, the multiplication tables, being in fact all rhythm and dramatic progression and design, are invitations to dance and make up plays and start geometric drawing. And every other piece of subject matter is approached in a way that allows it to yield up its soul-satisfying life.

Children heart-nourished by their learning remain heart-involved in their activities. They do not balk at even the least interesting housekeeping chores of home or schoolroom, but do them freely, from within, vigorously meeting the challenge of necessity.

Is it not to such as these that we may look for a heartfelt renewal of the social impulse that would let us do our work in life with love's enjoyment?

(1973)   Marjorie Spock

My thoughts are flying to school:
There will my body be trained
to rightful activity.
There will my soul be guided
To rightful life-strength.
There will my spirit be wakened
To rightful humanity.

Rudolf Steiner
(Translation, R. P.)

When the Bell Rings

To wonder at beauty,
Stand guard over truth,
Look up to the noble,
Decide for the good:
Leads man on his journey
To goals for his life,
To right in his duties,
To peace in his feeling,
To light in his thought,
And teaches him trust
In the guidance of God
In all that there is:
In the world-wide all,
In the soul's deep soil.

Rudolf Steiner
(Transl. Arvia McKaye Ege)

Gratitude ~ Love ~ Responsibility

The course of a human life falls roughly into two parts. In the beginning, till we reach adulthood. we are at the receiving end of life: parents. teachers, and society bestow their care upon us. Later follows the time when we ourselves are called upon to contribute to other people and to society. This is part of growing up, of maturing.

Think of the boundless expectations with which a young child anticipates his birthday or other gift-bestowing events, how he feels at the center of the world! Actually most of the early part of life is a continuous receiving. Later, the birthdays are no longer what they used to be, and the day often passes unnoticed by others. Obligations, instead of the former expectations, become dominant.

The receiving comes naturally; the giving has to be learned. Although they both interplay, there is a definite dividing line. This falls perhaps between romance and married life, and between being a student and taking on a job-responsibility. The transition we all have to make can either be hindered or helped, according to the education we have received.

There are many problems today. Often the growing-up process seems delayed. This shows up in the inability to make commitments to others, or to one's work. Irresponsibility is rampant, as we can read from many symptoms of the day, such as our rising divorce rate, the problem of deserted children, the appalling nursing-home situation, careless workmen, lack of work ethics, being on the take, or graft. The attitude of 'what's in it for me?' seems widespread. This self-centeredness may be proper for a young child but is misplaced in the adult, creating social ills and thereby affecting the lives of others adversely.

It seemed all so much easier in the past when methods of social indoctrination still worked, when norms of "good social behavior" were still drilled into children. "Being a lady", "being a gentleman", were well-defined norms that pre-established automatic lines of social behavior. You dressed in a certain way, spoke in a certain way, and your manners were determined by the customs of your social class. The further back we go, the more the playing a role was part of the social structure. This has broken down completely and is no longer part of the system of upbringing. It all seems to have started with the weakening of discipline in the raising of children.

Children are no longer formed from outside, but neither are they formed from within. How otherwise could we understand the symptoms of our amorphous teenagers who take on the mores and tastes of their peer-groups, imitating whatever is around them, their shapeless personalities without ideals and direction of their own? The fact that imitation, instead of self-direction, is so pronounced among adolescents raises an educational question. Was imitation, which is the learning mode of the very young child, given its proper due during the early childhood years? What did they imitate at home as young children?

Here we approach a sad chapter of upbringing today. The old norms are gone. Modern mothers seem often to be without instincts for the real needs of a young child. There are no traditions to fall back on, only uncertainty, at best, hopelessly unworkable theories about treating the child "as a person." You only need visit a modern home or observe a family meal—and you know it all!

"What would you like?" "What do you want?"—These questions in many variations form the atmosphere surrounding the young child. However well intended, the continuous catering to his wants acts as a poison to the young soul. It awakens premature consciousness of his likes and dislikes, his wants and don't-wants, as if these were of greatest importance to him and to others. They become an integral part of his vocabulary and of his responses at the dinner table, at getting dressed or going to bed, during leisure time, and in and out of school. The child becomes prey

25

to the whims of the moment: now I want to do it, now I don't want to do it! This forms hindrances in his social conduct and creates discipline problems, causing a bleak outlook for growing up.

In the very young child, the likes and dislikes may sound cute and amusing; in the long run, however, they breed the worst form of egotism, self-centeredness, and blindness to the needs of others or of a situation. They narrow down his interests to what rises within him at the spur of the moment. He may not feel like doing things that need to be done, resulting in lack of discipline on all fronts.

The consequences of this child-centered upbringing come to full force with the awakening of the critical faculties at puberty and during the stormy years of adolescence. They manifest themselves then as moodiness, arrogance, criticism, rejection, irresponsibility, raw egotism, doing things for kicks, or even vandalism and destructiveness. In milder forms they show up in the attitude of taking things continuously for granted, having things done for them, given to them, without appreciation or even awareness of the effort, the cost, the work, the source, the giver involved.

*

What then can be done? Should be done? If the forming from outside has become obsolete (although a modicum of courtesy and good manners should not be abandoned), can we help the child by other means to develop eventually into a mature, responsible person? And how can this be done?

Let us use an analogy: every gardener knows that in order to enjoy blossoms and fruits, careful early work is required in preparing the soil, planting the seeds, tending the growing plants. Roots, stems, and leaves need much care in order for blossoms to appear. Pruning may be necessary; insects and weeds must be eliminated.

Education, like gardening, is a life-process that requires time and care. Like the plant, the child goes through various phases of maturing; and the educator (the parents or teacher) can well be likened to a gardener who cannot harvest through neglect. The gardener will not be able to change a rose into a lily, but he can certainly, with the proper know-how, nurture the rosebush until it bears blossoms; and so can the educator aid the child to bring out his innate human qualities which, without adequate help, might suffer the fate of the rosebush that blooms sparsely or not at all.

We are now talking about the education of the moral life, not about intellectual training. And we have to look at it in three phases: the early childhood years, the elementary-school age, and adolescence. They relate to the growing child, just as the root, the stem with leaves, and the blossoms relate to the unfolding plant.

If the goal is responsibility, inner discipline, the willingness to do one's share, and eventually the ability to give oneself direction and purpose in life, the soil for this blossoming will have to be prepared early in life.

Responsibility grows out of love, which in turn has grown out of gratitude. Rudolf Steiner gave this sequence in an educational lecture in Holland, in 1924,* as the three soul-qualities to be fostered during the three phases of growing up: thankfulness during the years of the preschool child; love as the virtue for the elementary-school years; responsibility as the outgrowth of these qualities during the adolescent period.

If these concepts seem startling to begin with, they become ever so obvious to one working with children and reflecting upon life in general. Isn't thankfulness and appreciation the mother-soil for love? And then, doesn't genuine love, not infatuation, lead to the wish to reciprocate, to help, to do one's share? It is so in life, and it works also in the education of the child.

During the early years, when everything is given to the child and he is solely a recipient, isn't thankfulness the

---

* Rudolf Steiner, *Human Values in Education*. Ten lectures given in Arnheim, Holland, July 1924. Lecture Six. Rudolf Steiner Press, London, 1971.

natural response? Fortunate is the child who can learn early in life to bow his head in reverence and gratitude at the dinner table, while the family says grace; fortunate is the child who, before going to bed, is led to look up to the stars and the moon at night in thankfulness and security for their watching over him while he sleeps; fortunate is the child who is guided to speak a prayer in bed, in thankfulness for the varied gifts of the day; fortunate is the child who can even thank the sun for shining or the rain for watering the trees; fortunate is the child who can live in a family atmosphere where gratitude and appreciation are expressed for the work and care that father and mother contribute daily. Indeed, fortunate is the child who can thus imitate the very gestures and language of gratitude, thereby learning from early years to turn his attention to the source of the many and varied gifts of life, instead of concentrating on his own wants.

In the above-quoted lecture Rudolf Steiner summarized the child's need to experience thankfulness:

"Why does the child do this or that in the years before he is seven? Because he wants to imitate. He wants to do what he sees being done in his immediate surroundings. But what he does must be connected with life, it must be led over into living activity. We can do very much to help him bring this about if we accustom the child to feel gratitude for what he receives from his environment. Gratitude is the basic virtue in the child between birth and the change of teeth. If he sees that everyone who stands in some relationship to him in the outer world shows gratitude for what he receives from this world; if, in confronting the outer world and wanting to imitate it, the child sees the kind of gestures that express gratitude, then a great deal is done towards establishing the right human moral attitude. Gratitude is what belongs to the first seven years of life." (p. 125)

During times of loss and loneliness—times that will be encountered by everyone—it has become part of folk wisdom to learn to "count one's blessings." This means to find consolation by actively replacing self-pity with the feeling of gratitude for the gifts of life that remain. How much richer, happier, and more fulfilled the lives of our children could be if, instead of an impoverishing self-centeredness, their parents and teachers were to foster the life-habit of thankfulness for the many blessings around them, which otherwise remain unnoticed and unappreciated.

*

The cultivation of thankfulness should not cease with the elementary school years, but as the child becomes ready to leave the small family unit and go to school, a new learning force, beyond that of imitation, comes to the fore. "Do as I do" is gradually replaced by "love as I love". Love for learning and love for his teachers now expand his inner horizon. (However, premature schooling before the child is ready and longing for it, will certainly suffocate this love of learning.) Again, fortunate is the child who can learn from loving and enthusiastic teachers in an atmosphere of sympathy—from teachers who can open his soul to the beauty and wonders of nature, and to human achievements, struggles, and possibilities as they are depicted first in myths and legends, and later in historical figures. Fortunate is the child who can glow for heroes, legendary or historical, for their courage and their victories over adversity, who can identify with the good forces that prevail, and can develop antipathy for base deeds. A student who can react with anger and indignation, even outrage, to unjust or destructive actions as they have occurred in history, is well on his way towards responsibility. He will not tolerate destructiveness and irresponsibility in his environment, because moral feelings are implanted deeply within him.

Here we have to say a word about the prevalent indiscriminate television-viewing by children, where misfortune and destruction become funny and provide amusing entertainment. There the child lives in an amoral climate, his values become confused, his feelings callous, his responses paralyzed. Any parent who cannot see this detrimental influence on the moral development of a pliable, vulnerable child, *must* be blind.

But what about the child who displays amoral tendencies through his indifference towards good and evil, to whom all is the same, whose heart forces are inactive? Love cannot be taught directly. Rudolf Steiner, in the above-mentioned lecture, suggested that "if we perceive that what is good does not really please him, neither does what is bad awaken his displeasure . . . a knowledge of human nature will prevent us from setting about things in such a way that we say: this child is lacking in love for the good and antipathy for the bad. I must instill it in him! This cannot be done. But it will come about of itself if we foster gratitude in the child. It is therefore essential to know the part gratitude plays in the course of moral development in life." (Page 126)

Love grows out of gratitude; the feeling of responsibility, as the blossoming of the earlier stages, awakens with adolescence. Although there are some children who may show this quality in earlier years, they are the exception. This does not mean that, until it awakens, children should not be asked to do things, should have everything done for them—far from it!

*

Children love to participate. The toddler wants to be around his mother, yearns to imitate what she does, wants to do with her what she is doing. If she does not respond, but instead puts him out of her way, she is laying the foundation for no participation in the years to come. Parents create the situations in which they later find themselves. And if the teenagers still come to the table and leave the table without moving a finger to help, or sit in front of the television while mother slaves in the kitchen or is cleaning the house, these are only the natural consequences of her having put them out of her way (and in front of the box) in the first place. If instead, young children are permitted to be 'under foot', are encouraged to 'help' and to 'work' alongside the mother, at first in the spirit of imitative play, they will be happily engaged. In time their untrained fingers will become skillful, their clumsy hands become capable, and many of the tedious household chores can be accomplished cheerfully (remember, we are still in the imitative phase) together with the mother, and later alone. "Come and be my helper" should be the initial attitude towards establishing the family habit if everyone is to help, everyone is to participate.

Children who learn early to be useful, to do constructive work, to contribute in small and then in larger ways, having their work appreciated and valued, will not easily become discipline problems. But children who are non-participating, unoccupied, bored and ever dependent on stimulation from outside for entertainment, expecting constantly to have things done for them, will be far less cooperative at home and in school. And their path to maturity will be blocked by poor habits and attitudes.

*

Adolescence need not be a time of instability and confusion. It can be a period of learning, of intense idealism, of love for the whole world. A youth who has been taught in early childhood to look in thankfulness to the source of the many gifts of life, who has been guided during the school years to love the good and to abhor evil, will have a moral basis for his intellectual capacities and judgments as they awaken with puberty. He will be able to act and to judge out of his own insight, without the need to imitate his age-peers. He will also know his proper place in life, in proportion to other people's contribution. He will want to build upon, not tear down the work of others. He can look forward to the future, with all the idealism of youth, to the time when he will be able to make his contribution to society.

By way of gratitude and love, he will come to responsibility.

These are the goals for an education of the moral life, and reality will often fall short of the attainable ideals. But unless we know firmly the direction, we will never find the way.

(1976)   —Gisela T. O'Neil

Activity in Education

From time to time the educational world is swept by what are known professionally as "crazes". Briefly, a "craze" is a method of teaching which is thought by some to be the last word in enlightened and up-to-date education, and by others—well, just a craze. And the fact that this word is used chiefly by teachers themselves, and has originated from among them, allows one to use it here without implying any unworthy criticism.

One such craze which has been discussed with considerable vigor among teachers and in the educational press, goes by the name of 'activity'. Broadly speaking, activity means that the children are to be encouraged to do something in connection with what they learn. One might object, of course, that learning is itself alrady a "doing," an activity, and that the young child who has been asked, for instance, to find out how many 15 cent articles he can obtain for $1.05 already has plenty to do. But that isn't enough nowadays. You have to get hold of some real money (or a suitable educational counterfeit), and go to a real shop (or part of the school you have temporarily transformed into a shop) and actually buy $1.05 worth of 15 cent articles (even if the articles themselves are worthless or non-existent). And such a method, worked out in all sorts of ingenious ways for every subject, constitutes activity.

And there can be no doubt that it is a good method as methods go. Even Mr. Squeers knew and practiced it in his notorious academy at Dotheboys Hall, where it was his custom, having led the boys through the intricacies of spelling, to send them off to do something in connection with their studies. As he once explained to his newest teacher, Nicholas Nickleby, "W-I-N-D-E-R spells 'winder,' Nickleby; and when a boy knows that he goes and cleans 'em."

But once again one can see in this how a method, worked out by itself simply as a method, isn't necessarily educational; and the very fact that these methods, these "crazes" come and go, shows only too clearly that they fail to meet, or only partially meet the basic needs of the child. A method, any method, if it is to meet those needs must be based on a knowledge of the child. If that knowledge is incomplete or unsound, then the method must sooner or later break down and a new one be sought, which can rest securely on such knowledge.

It was to provide such a method, and to let the world test its practical application that Rudolf Steiner some forty-five years ago entered the sphere of public education, and out of a life's work devoted to the formulation of a comprehensive knowledge of the human being, gathered around him a group of teachers at the opening of the Waldorf School and gave them the leading thoughts for their work. And the first words he ever spoke to them were not about WHAT they were to teach, or even HOW they were to teach, but WHOM they were to teach—the child, the young human being. And that has continued to be one of the fundamental requirements, qualifications if you like, of all those who teach in Rudolf Steiner schools.

In every word Rudolf Steiner spoke, the fact that we have before us in the child a living spiritual being, active in every fiber of his organism, was never for one moment lost sight of; nor what must inevitably follow—that everything one does in the way of education and instruction must harmonize with the living, active individuality.

A child is so supremely and completely active that we hardly need to make him more active—even supposing we could; but we must know by what activity that which we have to give him is best mediated. We must know whether he is being too active in one direction and needs the compensating 'rest' of activity elsewhere; or conversely, whether he isn't active enough in one direction and needs stimulation. But just to consider activity in an abstract way or to consider only limb activity is just not enough. There is for instance the obvious activity of sense perception-cum-thinking, or intellectual activity, by which the major part of what we call learning is still acquired. There is the even more physical activity of the limbs by which all the skills of writing, drawing, etc. are practiced and developed. But there is also the tireless rhythmical activity of the breathing and circulation of the blood which must on no account be ignored, and what is perhaps even more subtle, what even more 'makes or mars' the child's future, that silent, mysterious activity of growth which accompanies the whole course of education.

It might be a surprise to some that the activity of breathing is something one should take into account in education—but a little thought on the matter should make the connection quite clear. Let us take, for instance, what is perhaps the most inactive lesson of all outwardly—that one where the child sits still and listens to a story; and whether he is enjoined or obliged to sit still beforehand or not, he will none the less do so if the story is well told. This apparent stillness is an illusion; for as the story unfolds the child's soul follows, responds to all the changing events it portrays. It is a living, active experience for him. To ignore such movements in the soul, or in other words, in the feeling-organisation of the child, is to blind oneself by force to some of the most vigorous activities in the child's life. Indeed, to fail to control such activities, by the way one tells such stories, stimulating here, quieting there, is to set up repercussions in the child's whole organism that may later have an effect on his outward, more apparent movements. Nor is the connection between these soul movements and actual physical movements so inscrutable as to escape detection by an observant teacher. Everyone knows how closely the feelings are connected with blood

34

circulation and breathing. Who has not himself suffered a shock of fear, and experienced afterwards those violent palpitations of the breathing and heavy hammerings of the heart? Or who has not at some time received unpleasant news and found the whole digestive system revolt at the thought of food, even to the point of actual vomiting. All the time a child is sitting "still" (and how still they can sit on such occasions) listening to a story, he is vigorously active, too, and those activities are re-echoed in the whole rhythmic system. This is so obvious that teachers must have noticed how a child is literally "tired" after having listened to an interesting story. Sometimes he will yawn prodigiously in order to restore the normal current of his breathing; invariably he will stretch himself; often, too, he will get violently active, repeating in actual physical movements and mimicry the incidents of the story, or breaking out into unrestrained and excited chatter. Then it is the time for him to play—to *rest* what has been so active in the soul by the release of activity elsewhere.

That activity which tires a child most quickly (a feeling for which is behind the popularity of the 'craze' outlined above) is the sense perception-cum-thinking, or intellectual activity. There was a time when this was considered almost the only activity required in education. Some of us can still remember the days when school was a place where you sat still, with your hands behind your back (*and* your feet together on the footrest) and listened to what the teacher told you and watched what he did on the blackboard. But almost everyone agrees today that this is wrong. It is extremely difficult—if not impossible—for even a fully mature adult to endure a long period absorbing knowledge in this way, and that it was ever demanded of little children shows us into what aberrations a short-sighted view of the child is likely to lead us. Have you not observed, for instance, a veritable ripple of relief pass across a whole audience, subtle but perceptible, when a lecturer or speaker in the midst of a closely reasoned discourse pronounces those welcoming words, "Now let me give an illustration . . . " and though he still continues to use words to speak, everyone rejoices that they can now rest one part of their listening soul and call into activity another—the imaginative, picture-forming capacity. Rudolf Steiner often speaks of 'humor' in the giving of a lesson, but he doesn't necessarily mean 'hearty laughter' (though that too has a most improtant place in the range of soul and physical activities), but those subtle fluctuation of mood, that breathing of the soul, that variation between the heavy, the tense, and that which relieves the tension. All this is activity—activity which the teacher must be able to stimulate and abate almost at will, and one which, properly directed, will keep the child keen and alert even though he may not be roaming round the class or going off on some cultural expedition in the neighborhood. If this is not done, then our teaching and we suffer that damning and crushing condemnation of the little girl who, on being asked what she had been doing at school replied, "Nothing. Teacher was talking all the time."

The trouble is, however, that when the evils of excess in one method have become apparent there is a danger to run into excess in another direction. "Let the children do it themselves" has become in some quarters a principle of modern education, and if this goes on unchecked we shall rapidly approach the anomalous position where, instead of teachers teaching the children, we shall have the children teaching the teachers. It is thought now by some that children should talk freely, roam about the classroom, do this or that as their inclination dictates, and the teacher should be hardly much more than an observer taking his cue as to method from what the children do themselves. But if the teacher secedes from his natural authority, if he fails to guide the child's activities out of his knowledge of those activities and how they originate, the children must grow up with a casualness and dilettantism which will be hard to uproot later.

That this should be possible is all the more strange when it is remembered that in that one sphere of a child's total activity, where his own initiative might be given almost unrestricted free play, he is still bound down to the most rigid observance of a strict form,—to wit, in his play. A sports teacher is as essential a member of the staff nowadays as a teacher of arithmetic, and no local authority would any more think of putting up a new school without a playing field than they would leave out a cloakroom. In that part of its activity where a child is by nature prone to express himself freely (and where we can learn a great deal by becoming a mere observer), he now tends to be organized and supervised out of all recognition. Any child will naturally kick, throw and hit a ball, and unite with his fellows to do so, and the ingenuity of children in devising games for themselves (some of which have persisted down the centuries) is well-known, but one cannot help wondering how far children by themselves would have got in devising all the complicated forms of leagues, league tables, cup-ties, championships and point systems into which their purely physical activities tend to be directed nowadays. It is a sad confession of much modern educational theory (even though the principle by which it exists is supported by the dignity of a Latin tag—*Mens sana in corpore sano*) that what a child loses in physical well-being through having to sit in school and learn, must be made up for by a vigorous imitation of adult pastimes on the playing field and nowhere is the so loudly trumpeted freedom of modern education so sadly lacking as in the child's play.

A human being is already an essentially active being and does not need to be made so by education. We can no more import activity into education than we can hope to make the ocean wet by pouring water into it. But we can strain the activities that are already there by too much use, or cause others to atrophy through refusing to recognize them or by failing to give them the opportunity to develop. And that the supremest activity to which all education is directed, that which alone gives us the right and reason to educate at all, the unfolding in full self-consciousness of the free, independent human spirit, can only appear long after our efforts are over, and will be the final judge of all we do. Education exists for no other purpose than to guide the activities of the natural child that are already there, so that the free spirit may awake in due time in full consciousness of its power and activity.

(1963)   Alan Howard

(Reprinted with the kind permission of "Child and Man", publication of the Rudolf Steiner Schools in England.)

The Effect Of Waldorf Education On Home Life

When a friend of our family called to ask me if I would write an article on the effect of Waldorf education on our home life, I said yes, mainly because I could not think of a convincing, polite way to say no. I was plagued by doubts; after all, we weren't anthroposophists, I wasn't a writer, and our family life had its ups and downs. Yet Waldorf education as we came to know it did and does have a profound and continuing effect on our family. I decided to take the plunge and began to sort out and recreate our changing view of ourselves and our children. We have three, a girl of ten and two boys, five and eight.

We had always felt that a family living in the mainstream of modern culture must continually redefine and rediscuss what is healthy for a growing child and the family. Our own upbringing and the things we saw happening all around us, did not provide an example or guide for what we wanted: a strong family working together.

The search for creating such an ideal found no answers in our own experience. When our first child learned to speak, we tended to fall into the pattern in which a child is assessed in the modern culture: the smarter she was, the happier we were. The more she "knew", the prouder we got. I'm astonished now to think that we taught her the entire alphabet at 21 months! We hung letters and numbers all around her room, provided her with Sesame Street, flash cards, books and lots of positive feedback for being a bright little girl. Since she was eager to please us, she learned it all.

When our older children were approaching school age we decided on private school mainly because of my husband's disillusionment with the public schools he had formerly taught in. We also felt we should cooperate as much as possible with any school we chose. It happened to be a Waldorf school. That was the beginning—our children, the school and its parent-workshops slowly gave us a new direction and gradual certainty on how to create a family atmosphere in which we could all prosper.

In a rough sort of way the following categories stand out in my mind as the clearest way to talk about this.

Religion

Religion in our own upbringing was experienced as sterile and hypocritical. Our initial attitude had been that it is better to do nothing. There was, however, a gnawing feeling that we would have to face this issue once the children grew older. That first year at Green Meadow we seemed to whiff some kind of spiritual point of view; it helped raise our own doubts about whether it is really possible to do nothing. Laura and Daniel would come home from school and in their wonderful innocence proceed: "Do you want to hear what we say before snack?"

Then they would say this prayer:

> *Earth who gave us all this food,*
> *Sun who made it ripe and good,*
> *Dearest Earth and dearest Sun,*
> *We'll not forget what you have done.*

They said it as though it belonged to them. We reflected on our own childhood where thoughts about food seemed to center on the fact that people were starving all over the world so we had better finish every bit!

Their prayer hit us as something that could be meaningful to us. For us as a family it seemed right. Our children also suggested we add candlelight to the evening meal and a family tradition became established. Our youngest child chimed right in, imitating the mood. Friends who join us for dinner and notice the candles and the care usually ask, "What's the occasion?" And someone always explains, "Oh, we do this every night."

There are several practical benefits to recreating the dinner hour; a prayer and candles seem to calm everybody down and make conversation easier, it distinctly sets this time apart as special and gives a sort of elegance to the simplest meal.

In a seminar for mothers we received more practical suggestions. With lots of fresh memories of the cajoling and struggles at bedtime we perked up our ears at suggestions as to how to create atmosphere for the children in the evening. We learned to use a candle instead of an electric light, to speak softly (this is still sometimes difficult) and to say with each child the evening prayer and perhaps sing a song or two. Besides giving the child the assurance of *his* time alone with the parent it provides a wonderful hidden benefit: all the little problems and hurts that would well be lost or overlooked in the daily hustle and bustle seem to come out at this time. One of our boys holds a lot in and he especially seems to use this quiet, safe time just to talk.

We needed the children to be our vehicle, but we became receptive to the gifts they brought to us from school, particularly a sense of wonder at the order of things. The children would come home with their stories of the seasons, each year the same cycle. There is order in nature and there is order in the heavens. As a family we learned to experience together the wonder of things.

It's difficult to describe the impact the third grade Old Testament block had on our daughter and our family. She lived into these stories in such a way that her descriptions of the glorious battles, struggles, sacrifices, and moral dilemmas of the ancient peoples were simply thrilling for her and an eye opener for us. These deep moral questions were so real for her we began to think of the Bible in a different way too. In fact, we had given our family Bible to a friend on "permanent loan" and had to ask for it back. We still laugh when we remember having to explain to our daughter that the Philadelphia *Phillies* did not mean the Philadelphia *Philistines*.

We got her a large print Bible at her request last Christmas and found her reading it with the fervor she now gives the Nancy Drew series. It seemed to us that through these stories the school had tapped something very fundamental in her at just the right age. Our boys look forward to this block because she explained to them that although she could tell them some of the stories, her teacher advised that they must be a little older to hear all of them . . . what a wonderful thing to look forward to.

Participation in Family Work

For us there was no real precedent for teaching responsibility and participation. In most homes, the parents wait until the son or daughter is almost grown up—as happened in my own life—until the suggestion comes that the daughter should perhaps vacuum her own room and make her bed. There seems to be a custom of one caregiver per family while the children occupy themselves elsewhere.

At a parent workshop it became clear that many of us wanted a family that worked together, but we really didn't know how one goes about doing that. We learned that several things were essential, attitude, investment of time, and some creative thinking. Having the right attitude simply means that you believe that children really want to help and participate. It also means that one does not abruptly announce, "There's going to be some big changes around here!" It's a gradual process, and parents must be willing to help and guide, especially at first, and be prepared for constant backsliding. It became painfully clear to us that it took an awful lot of time to teach a child how to make his bed and to make sure he did it every day. We also began to think together about what a child could realistically be expected to do and at what age. Six-year-olds can fold and put away their laundry; even four-year-olds can do a pretty good job cleaning up their rooms. The older ones learn that jobs in the garden or with the horses take effort but have rewards.

Vacuuming, setting and clearing the table, changing their beds—this all belongs to participating in a family. The fruits of this are manifold. Children are proud of things they can do, it expands their confidence in their own capacities, and the process itself teaches the consequences that occur when work is left undone. This is especially true if one has animals: a dog left unfed remains just that in spite of the most imaginative excuse.

These are all lessons of life, learned naturally through participating in family work. We found it useful to be willing to say sometimes, "I'll help you do it."

Lest this all sound too rosy and pat, let me add that reminders are still essential in our home and probably always will be.

Use of Free Time

My first thought about use of free time is television. Much has been written about this lately and many people in the wider culture are taking a second and third look at the whole question. We all know Waldorf schools do not recommend TV for children, especially little ones. Our family gradually got the message and turned off the TV about three and a half years ago. In a nutshell, we came to see it as an essentially passive activity that was a poor substitute for experience. It is also a theft of time.

In the past I had found that when our children started to fight or I needed some quiet, I relied on TV. Instead of involving myself in the family situation, I escaped it by turning on the box. The implications both for myself and the children made me uncomfortable.

Once the TV gets turned off there is more time. Time for what? We realized that we really didn't quite trust our children's capacity to find things to do—in essence, to be children. However, it became quickly evident the children at Waldorf schools know how to play. Our children, especially the boys, play outside in *all* kinds of weather (this really is no problem if a child is properly dressed). The older ones read and we have a "project table" that always has fresh paper, beeswax, crayons, and puzzles on it. This is used every single day by our children and/or the neighborhood children. It seems to be a great unwinder after the long bus ride home.

As a family without TV, we are forced to interact more and have begun taking hikes, camping, and skating together. We also play board games. Our daughter spends time playing the 'cello and piano.

We have also come to appreciate *what* the children play with. Those beautiful wooden toys at school are a sharp contrast to the gimmicky dead-end things that never seem to last more than a week or two. It made sense to invest in some really good toys that were nice to look at, handle, and really lasted. At preschool workshops we saw that toys should be open-ended, not too strictly defined. A doll that does "everything" leaves a child little room to make it come alive and cuts off all the wonderful possibilities one may dream up.

The other thing we do in our free time is nothing. Just a lot of space for someone to tell you a story if he feels like it, take a walk, or watch the birds on the feeder outside.

Food

As in the case of television, many people in the wider culture are taking a second and third look at the food we eat.

The word "healthfood" seems like it should be a contradiction in terms, but both my husband and I began to rethink this whole area about ten years ago.

We were immediately at home with the school's attitude that it really matters what you eat and good wholesome unfooled-with food is always preferable.

There is a conscious effort to keep school-provided snacks as natural as possible and our littlest child already seems to sense what is really good to eat.

It was the children who explained what millet was, how to grind grain, and how good it is to pull a carrot out of the earth and pop it in your mouth. We had never really given much thought to the actual relationship between what we eat and the earth, rain and sun.

Now each Spring especially our oldest boy announces, "Let's plant a garden."

Conclusion

Our last child was born just about the time we entered the school and has really benefited most from the education. As his parents, our view is hardly unbiased, but he seems to have such a bright, loving, enthusiastic approach to life that it continually reaffirms for us some of the choices we have made.

I see that each year at the school has made us conscious of more possibilities. As all five of us get older, it may be that this process will just continue.

(1978)   —Ruth McArdle

Pressure and the Spirit of Play

Every school represents a continuation, but also a critique, of the society of which it is a part. Teachers are partly transmitters, partly reformers, of their culture. So it is, too, with Waldorf and Rudolf Steiner School teachers. At times some of us may seem critical, causing uneasiness in those who would like to feel that our civilization is progressing satisfactorily. Yet, although our criticisms must occasionally stress the negative, their intent is positive. We do think reformation necessary, but our goal is renascence.

I have on other occasions spoken about the fact that our age lives under heavy pressures that exploit man and nature alike. A man from another planet, by observing conditions in an average school, could easily guess the state of the culture at large. Perhaps most notable about American students just now is the fact that their childhood is being shortened. Their teeth are changing earlier than they used to; they are maturing earlier sexually; they adopt grownup modes of dress and behavior sooner; and they are playing serious baseball, football, and basketball before they reach their teens. It seems generally true, too, that the aptitude for abstract thinking is developing precociously.

The curriculum of the modern school is partly following, partly causing this trend to abandon childhood as soon as possible. Witness the demise of fairy tales and the introduction of reading—even of arithmetic and science—in kindergartens. Witness high school subjects shunted into the elementary school, and college subjects into high school. Consider the tactics of advanced placement, the ungraded high school as newly proposed, and the lengthening school year. Many of these impatient schemes betray the feeling that carefree youth, which would live for the sake of living, must hasten to leave its toys and joys, and take up tools for a life that is Serious Business.

One symptom of modern education is especially striking. This is the mania for swift reading. Children are encouraged, not to say harassed, to read ever faster and faster, as if academic progress were primarily a race with time, and speed of reading the very key to winning this race. In many thousands of children and parents the academic race is inspiring near-panic.

There is no doubt that the pressures of adult anxiety are shortening childhood, and squeezing it besides. These pressures move down from the level of national policy which insists upon a moon-shot day after tomorrow, to the nursery level, where parents with an eye on college insist upon their children 'learning' something. The child is asked to absorb more knowledge, and absorb it faster, regardless of his appetite. He must appear to be a thinker, long before experience can have ripened any real kind of thinking in him. Can we wonder that the knowledge of such children is joyless, and their thinking is powerless, when the children themselves have had so little part in developing either?

* * *

But now I would speak of that which is capable of withstanding every pressure: namely, the spirit of play. The curriculum and methods of the Waldorf schools have the avowed purpose of fostering this very spirit of play, for in it we see not only the great need of young people today, but an antidote for the distemper of our age.

We know that play characterizes childhood. Less often do we think of it as being also the signature of maturity. Yet Christ was speaking of the mature human being when he said, "Except . . . ye become again as little children, ye shall not enter the kingdom of heaven." Reflection upon this saying can bring one to the thought that Christ's admonition might be paraphrased: "Except in the spirit of play we will not realize the divine in ourselves, find the divine in the world, or participate worthily in the divine work of creation."

46

The child at play, the mature man who has risen to child-likeness, is 'in the world but not of the world.' He is close enough to shape things, yet free enough that his shaping fantasy may remain true to its own promptings. Nietzsche said that man passes, on his way to freedom, through three stages: the camel that asks to be heavily laden with rules and plans and duties given by the world, the lion that fights against the world for his freedom, and finally the child, who in mastery of the world possesses freedom and knows what to do with it.

Schiller in his *Letters on the Aesthetic Education of the Human Being* put the matter drastically but truly when he said: ". . . man only plays when in the full meaning of the word he is a man, and he is only completely a man when he plays." Schiller saw the thinking man bewitched by logic, the feeling man tossed by passion, the working man chained to fact. All these functions must be performed by man, but they are not exercised freely until the spirit of play finds its way into them. Play transforms the logical faculty into creative imagination. Play makes work that deadens, into art that enlivens. Play sets aside the storm and stress of passion for the quiet sense of freedom in which love unfolds.

The power of play mediates in perfect freedom between inner life and outer life. As the heart beats between the upper and the lower body, the spirit of play holds forth between conceptual necessities in the inner life of thought and practical facts in the outer life of action.

It is often assumed that while play occupies itself with unrealities, coping with reality requires work. Our habit of thought assigns play to children, work to adults. Were grown men and women permitted to regard life as, in the last analysis, a matter of play, we fear they would cease forthwith to be responsible. The exact contrary, however, may be argued. For the ideal of play which childhood holds out to the mature man is actually more serious than work. Play, as Schiller conceived it, is a whole-souled exercise of the human entelechy, whereas in work much of the soul may remain unenlisted. Play is a more complete undertaking than work, for play uses all our faculties, work only some. In play we ourselves lead. In work we are being pushed.

Our work becomes play to the extent that our own initiative completely cancels external pressure, and our love of action makes light of duty. The art of life, therefore, consists in transforming work into play. We should 'play the game,' not in the sense of 'playing along,' but in the sense of knowing the rules, accepting them gladly, and then plunging into the sport for the joy it gives. Under these circumstances we see that true play develops a more complete sense of responsibility than work, since in play we say 'I will,' while in work we can only say 'I must.'

Play enriches life, work impoverishes it; for in play, being is fulfilled; in work, being is frustrated. The energy for play is self-sustaining and self-renewing; for work, the energy that is spent must be drawn from somewhere else. Is it not clear, then, that the enjoyment, gratitude, and free activity which we have been calling play stands closer to a sound education, sound health, and sound economy than the unloved necessity, the pressure, which goes by the name of work?

Waldorf school methods in nursery and kindergarten try to establish the fully active, fully creative spirit of play so firmly that it will set the tone for the rest of life. Waldorf parents know how in the early years letters, numbers, and skills, literature, science, and history put down their first roots in the spirit of play. They are presented imaginatively. They awaken free interests. They lead to creative art. It is not my present purpose, however, to review Waldorf school methods, but to stress values that should be honored in every school. Does not the very health of Western society ask us to remit the pressures of selfish purpose and materialistic desire that now exploit men and nature? Could not happier, more lasting contributions be made from the spirit of play? Society would undoubtedly prosper, were ordinary men and women educated to live their lives more creatively, with more fantasy, which they *can* do when they are not too abstracted from the earth as intellectuals, nor too gripped by it as breadwinners.

One can believe that the intuitive sense so closely bound up with the spirit of play is able, if given the chance, to bring about many changes. For example, the farmer who began to imagine how things look from the viewpoint of his apple trees and earthworms, his cows and his chickens, would surely move away from many practices that the short-sighted profit motive has introduced into agriculture. And the spirit of play appearing in such imaginative identification would not only enhance the life of creatures on the farm: how it could improve relationships between human beings, too—between age and youth, man and woman, black and white, Easterner and Westerner!

Imagine for a moment an injection of the spirit of play into business. What is closer to play than the making, transporting and trading that we call 'the economy'! These actions and transactions are said to be done to *earn* a living. But they already *are* living. They spring from zest for life. Wages are necessary, but work *is* done by healthy men and women in any case. They care primarily for the pleasure of being active at tasks that interest them. They want the humor, the warmth, the vitality, of companionship with their fellow-workers. They love the sense of an importance, however modest, in the scheme of things. They look forward to testing themselves against life and bringing forth their resources to meet its challenges. Were the mainspring of all this adult busy-ness recognized as actually the instinct for play, the game would find ways to make itself more clearly worth playing for its own sake. Then wages could find their proper place. We may expect that when management no longer sees profit as its main goal, labor will not fight so single-mindedly for 'more'.

Again, if scientists were to pursue their studies in Schiller's spirit of play, would not the methods and the findings of science change remarkably? It seems to me that a more heartfelt wonder would replace our mental curiosity. Also, the using of knowledge solely for the purpose of capturing material power would decline, as the spiritual power of being flowed from nature to the natural scientist in his cognition. The perceived world, which has grown so absolutely material only because we are so positively hardheaded in our search for knowledge, will begin to relax, letting us feel the being within the seeming. New powers of inquiry, indeed, could arise, able to roll the stone of dead fact away from the grave in which we have for a long time now laid the world spirit.

If our scientists would hold to the fact that true science is but a form of play, they could begin to lift their noses from the grindstone of analysis. They could look up and about them, drawing together things far and near, subtle and obvious, inner and outer. The multiplication of exclusively physical detail, which is exhausting our capacity for wonder and blockading our path towards wisdom, would be subdued and contained within a stronger sense of the whole.

The spirit of play could bring light again into religion. In this spirit men and women would feel closer to the all-fashioning Creator than they can do when their concept of God is based upon speculations that ask too much after judgment and purpose. What is the 'purpose' of trout in a mountain stream, of birds that give voice to the crystal air, of jungle tigers burning bright? Nature is a work of art; its forms are all fantasy. Is it not difficult to conceive that pheasants and woodchucks, dandelions and geraniums could be the handiwork of a deity motivated by what we call purpose?

What is true of the religious feeling for nature may be true also of the religious sense for destiny. Shakespeare is echoing what we know of destiny from our own dreams, when he says that "all the world's a stage" whereon we play our parts. Melville imagined the Fates as stage managers. One may venture, therefore, that a role-playing imagination will be of more help in answering the questions of destiny than will legalistic ideas of punishment and reward. Fate may unfold according to necessities better sensed by the playwright than by pedagogue or judge.

Speaking of jurisprudence, I must say that I have wondered at times whether justice could not be meted out to criminals more imaginatively, or as I might say now, playfully. At present we seem so often to ignore what no playwright or child at play would overlook: namely, the actual relationships of destiny between the criminal and his victim. Judgment rendered out of a feeling for dramatic justice could certainly touch the heart of the wrong-doer in ways inaccessible to legal judgments.

I cannot leave out of consideration the benefits to be expected in a culture that would rightly value play, without alluding to what has happened to recreation and amusement in our present culture. By subordinating the play motif so conscientiously, we have arrived at a situation in which life has lost its savor. We try to renew this savor through sensation, but the thrills available to our mundane spirit have lost their innocence and do not satisfy. How could they?

It is really not thrills we desire, but fun; really not escape, but buoyancy. But the conversion of adults, who should know better, into playboys will not really be checked by anything less powerful than the spirit of play.

In conclusion I should like to say a word about one of many ways in which a rightly-cultivated sense of play might affect human health. Let us look at the heart.

It is well known that diseases of the circulatory system, particularly of the heart, constitute in our country the greatest single threat to health. *The World Book* estimates that this type of ailment doubly outweighs, as a cause of death, the next five diseases combined. According to Dr. Paul Dudley White, the statistics show that, for heart disease, America has the distinction of being about the most unhealthful country in the world. Mortality from this cause is still increasing and is said to be appearing some ten or twelve years earlier in each successive generation.

What have pressures and play to do with the heart? Among the causes of illness usually mentioned is the swift pace of modern life. This it is that brings disorder into the circulatory system. Remedy: we should be less active. But on the other hand, we hear that the trouble results from our sedentary habits: we should be more active. Or again, diet is to blame: we should eat less of animal fats. Worry is bad: we may require tranquillizers. And, of course, since the disposition to heart disease is to some extent hereditary, those who wish to avoid this kind of thing should use extreme care in the selection of their grandparents!

Dr. Hans Selye's famous research into the effects of stress on the human organism seems to support what we could guess: namely, that in a culture where freedom and fulfillment, love and joy, harmony and peace are prospering, there will be no epidemic of heart attacks. Where initiative is cramped, where pressures crowd in, where enjoyment is superficial and fulfillment is indefinitely postponed, men and women will find their burdened hearts faltering.

It seems to me that our American hearts are being squeezed from above and below. The drive towards intellectualism that starts—to speak only of the effects of formal education—in most elementary schools with the very first grade must surely tighten our children and stiffen them at the same time. The ever-increasing mechanization of the environment must contribute its further share. And then, the urgent hurry, the bitter competition, that would have us force the blood past vessels already tightened!

It seems to me that we are living harder and enjoying it less as the years go by. But blood springs to its tasks when the inner man feels free and in his freedom conceives enthusiasm for life. That students today are falling short of such vividness may be read in the voice that can no longer reach the high notes, in the gait that drags, in the slump that has replaced sitting, in the sunken chests found even among athletes, and in the general inability shown by young people on the stage to portray characters of abounding humor, magnanimous spirit, or marked vitality.

Reform that leads to renascence must start in education. Many a teacher today would be glad to pioneer in replacing extrinsic with intrinsic values, and in the Waldorf School we have already gone comparatively far in this direction. But teachers need the support of parents. Parents could scarcely be better placed than they are, to understand why a revolt against pressure is overdue, and why the spirit of play should lead this revolt. They need only look around and into themselves.

(1963)   —John F. Gardner

II

THE WALDORF KINDERGARTEN

A child's world is new and fresh and beautiful, full of wonder and excitement. It is our misfortune that for most of us that clear-eyed vision, that true instinct for what is beautiful and awe-inspiring is dimmed and even lost before we reach adulthood. If we had influence with the good fairy who is supposed to preside over the christening of all children, I should ask that her gift to each child in the world be a sense of wonder so indestructible that it would last throughout life, as an unfailing antidote against the boredom and disenchantment of later years, the sterile preoccupation with things that are artificial, the alienation from the sources of our strength.

Rachel Carson

Kindergarten in the Rudolf Steiner School

Most of our children no longer live, as in the olden days, on large farms where, with their numerous brothers and sisters, they helped their mother in the house and their father and the farm hands in the barns and fields. They loved their pets. They helped care for cows and horses, pigs and poultry, and shared in the thrilling activities of seed time and harvest. In the evenings, they used to play by the fireside or listen to stories told by parents or neighbors or by strangers welcomed to their hospitable hearths.

This sort of life, of course, offered a most natural and healthful growing toward the time when a child can safely begin to use his thinking powers at the age of six or seven years. For a child who is lucky enough to have a joyful, natural family life, this would be the ideal moment to start going to school.

However, in these days, our strenuous, high-geared city life—with its small families, broken families, where grown-ups are in business and often away from home—has robbed our children of that natural way of living, that chance to learn wholesomely by "imitation and example". These are Rudolf Steiner's "magic words" for the way a little child should learn during his first six or seven years. He pointed out that though it is quite possible for a child to think and use his memory before this time, his later life will be more normal and healthy, if in his early years his forces are allowed to pour into just growing, if his "learning" is allowed its natural development through imitation.

But for this natural process of just growing, and of learning by imitation and example, there must be a rich background of things to imitate and a health-giving environment. And so the kindergarten in a Rudolf Steiner School is not a sort of lower first grade where "learning" as such is started. Instead, it tries to give the little children as much as possible of that experience and background which our modern way of living has taken away from them.

Though our seeds must be planted in pots of earth on a sunny window sill, these little gardens are cared for and watered each day (sometimes even to the point of destruction). The children play with their barn and tiny toy animals on the floor; the surrounding hedges and fences and churches and villages are all made of oddly shaped and varicolored blocks gathered here and there from left-overs in the carpenter shops of friends. We find that the geometric, rigid forms of the usual commercial blocks have a crystallizing effect on the imagination and offer few possibilities for building. On the other hand, the varied, more or less fluid curves and sizes and clear colors of our blocks suggest infinite possibilities and stimulate the imagination to vast heights of creativeness. For "the work of the imagination moulds and forms the brain."

We have our housework, too, taking turns on each of the jobs. It may be more fun to feed the fish and water the plants than to mop the floor, but we "take it as it comes"—as the mother sheep said to her lambs about the different kinds of grass.

When the time comes for mid-morning lunch, though it be only cold water in a paper cup and a crisp graham cracker, we eat together at a long family table, made by joining several small ones, and each child takes his special place. We take turns choosing the center piece: plant or gold-fish bowl. We wait until the one, whose day it is, comes to pass the cracker basket to each of us, *at the left side;* we fold our hands while we say our verse. After lunch we have our story. The resting time comes when needed and the children lie still and listen to quiet music.

More chances to *share* and *take turns* come during the outdoor playtime and we try to take the consequences of our own deeds as soon as they come into being, in order to learn the reaction of the world before the world gives it to us, as Dr. Steiner once suggested.

We try to bring the whole being into action in all we do, from eurythmy to telling fairy tales. We must always remember that in artistic activity the whole being actually does come into play. A phlegmatic and melancholic child is helped by an overabundance of outgoing, artistic expression such as musical activity, singing and painting. The choleric and sanguine children need the more formative, unifying qualities acquired in modeling, drawing and handwork. Eurythmy also is used to help in balancing temperamental difficulties and can be adapted at any moment to suit the immediate need. "However great the need for improvement the teacher may find in the child, he will not fail to see, in existing things themselves, the embryo of the future. At the same time he knows that in all things becoming, there must be growth and evolution. Hence he will perceive in the present the seeds of transformation and of growth. He invents no programs—he reads them out of what is there. What he thus reads becomes in itself a program, for it bears in itself the essence of development. From the nature of the evolving human being, the proper point of view for education will result. Perhaps the hardest task a kindergarten teacher has is to help the children who suffer from extremes of temperament, to acquire self-control, or some balance in them. Nor can anything give a teacher greater comfort than an appreciable degree of success in this high adventure." (*A Modern Art of Education* by Rudolf Steiner).

A few observations of children, known during my years of kindergarten teaching, will help to illustrate these words.

One child of five years, rather pale, with long, brown braids, slow, plodding, *phlegmatic*, overmeticulous, large for her age, often sat by herself playing with her own separate treasures, hoarding and satisfied. She had some of the qualities of a setting hen. She was comfortable and placid. But she was not out-going enough nor wide enough awake for her own good. Very soon the younger children and the high-strung ones (cholerics), and timid ones (melancholics) came closer under her wing in the free play time. The teacher always tried to keep her *bodily active* and gave her chances for *daring* to overcome her over-meticulousness. She became more friendly, almost motherly, and began to sparkle. She became happier and more active and noticeably popular with all the children. She was always pleased to be a "special helper".

Then there was a tall, thin, pale, little boy of four with very light hair and almost translucent skin, an extreme *choleric-sanguine* temperament. He had strangely beautiful eyes and an imagination which showed him more than most could see. He had an irregular life at home and never knew where he was to go or what to do after kindergarten hours. He was insecure, lonely and hungry for his mother. He was very loving. On the other hand, he was destructive and had terrific fits of temper amounting almost to frenzy, during which a veil of hardness would come over his eyes. At such times his teacher could not look at him directly or make demands of him, but quietly taking firm hold of his wrist, seeming to be unconcerned, talking to the other children as occasion demanded, she would assume that he was going to do what was required of him and then leave him alone to do it. During his two and one half years in the kindergarten this always succeeded. After a while he would quietly creep back into the group and then and only then would be accepted by the others. After one of those tantrums had been conquered the teacher would ask him to do some extra task alone, which would help him to grow whole again. While acting in fairy tales this child became transformed—noble and poised in the part of the golden prince and would conquer *any* dragons. He was given both parts in the little plays—king and prince, which he found difficult in daily life—dragon, witch and mischief maker, which he most easily lived. With the first, he conquered his difficulties; with the second, he became horribly bored and wanted to give it up! These successes even helped him to control his unfortunate elimination habits which had been caused by his emotional instability.

A little, light haired three-year-old-boy, with healthy body and beautifully formed head had not had much attention nor the usual regularity at home because of the busy life his family led. He had a high-pitched voice, was tense, had moments of being a little tired and wistful, but was one of the friendliest and happiest little boys ever known in our kindergarten. He was the perfect *sanguine* type. He would come forward with smiling eyes and hand outstretched to greet everyone. He learned to play quietly by himself when necessary, just waiting for whatever was to happen next—a needed peaceful time without too many impressions. He sang all our songs either with us or by himself with utter joy and no self-consciousness. The scattered attention of this little sanguine child was creatively taken up by our many group activities, whereas when left alone his concentration would be short and more turned in on himself.

There was a tiny, fragile, delicate-featured little girl four and a half years old, with large, brown eyes and dark, curly braids. Her temperament was *melancholic*. She was very exact, overcautious, overconscientious and her muscles were tense. She had younger sisters for whom she probably felt too responsible and so at school she was given little responsibility. She craved approval eagerly but shyly and the teacher often gave her a secret, special smile of encouragement. In the music time, the teacher could make an example of her ability for the class. Mostly through music and eurythmy and fairy tales, she blossomed into a freer, happier little being, more naturally sanguine—which is the most normal state for a child.

Another little girl of four came to our school one day, a few weeks after the fall term started. She had an upright carriage with firmly built body, round, blue eyes and a sensitive mouth, which turned down at the corners at the slightest rebuff. She had had few children to play with and had been surrounded by adoring relatives and nurses all her short life. This was her first experience away from home. She cried almost incessantly for the first week or two of school. She called for her nurse who, she evidently thought, would drop out of the sky on demand. The teacher required silence from her only during the morning verse and mid-morning lunch—otherwise, she appeared to ignore her. It was hard on the others but they played the game and carried on as usual. Her cries continued: "I want a drink of water. I want a drink of water. I want a drink of water. I want my nurse to give it to me." Teacher: "Your nurse won't be here until twelve o'clock. Would you like a drink of water?" She: "I'm not a bit thirsty, thank you." Teacher: "Very well." After days of seeing the other children put their hands over their ears and hearing them say, "She's a cry baby," spaces developed between her sobs and outcries. Gradually she began to observe and absorb what was going on about her, but she would not join in. During music and eurythmy, she would keep rhythm with her foot or head unless she saw someone watching her. At last her eyes began to smile at her teacher once in awhile. Then the teacher occasionally took her outside the room for a few moments and held her in her lap and listened to outpourings of talk about home. They had become fast friends.

After ten days, when she heard the two notes on the piano—the signal for "circle"—she came to the teacher and took her hand to join in. But she still resisted new things a little longer. By the end of three weeks she had accepted every activity but one, the one to mean more to her, eventually, than anything else—eurythmy. This she accepted only after Christmas. By the fourth week she came each day with glowing face and a more than friendly "good morning" to all. But even then remarks of the other children like: "It's nice here now, isn't it? Mary doesn't cry any more"—made the corners of her mouth droop and the teacher would hurry to say: "Oh, no, that was long ago, that's all over now." Then Peter: "But why did she cry? That's 'silly business'!" Teacher: "Don't you remember when you came last year and you didn't know us very well?" Peter: "But I didn't cry like *that*." Teacher: "No, you cried your kind of cry." Mary looked relieved at that. Peter looked a little sheepish and stopped arguing. Instead, he took Mary and led her toward the colored blocks. "Will you make a castle with me?" he asked. Then she was glad for she had always admired Peter.

Peter's cry when he was new at school had been loud enough but short lived, not stubborn like Mary's. He was a happy, outgoing, friendly child, very large and strong for his age. His occasional bursts of temper would have been less frequent if he could have had contact and competition with children equal to him in physical health and vigor. He was *sanguine* with occasional choleric spurts. It was a great help to both Peter and Mary to have to share and to have to conform to the general rhythm of the kindergarten day. Each of them, being an only child, had lived with grown-ups and had too much adult attention.

Mary, after six months of school knew just what everybody else should do and was in danger of being overhelpful, almost "bossy", especially to the little boy sitting near her on the other side of the playhouse.

He was Jonathan, three and a half years old, sturdy, healthy, with rosy cheeks. Explosively *choleric*, he was easily diverted by being swept into the group of the older children whom he unconsciously adored. The teacher often started some "group activity" for such moments—something really creative for him to imitate. One of the things he liked to imitate was painting and he would often sit quite peacefully with his three bowls of clear colors, "fire color", "shining sun color" and "sky blue", for half an hour at a time entirely oblivious of the others. "Softly, softly," with his big brush he would paint a whole paper fiery red, his cheeks aglow with the joy of it. The other children were just as pleased with his painting as he was and they came to warm their hands over it. His absorption and achievement in painting helped him to find himself, while the group activities taught him sociability. It was a good experience for both Mary and Jonathan to be near each other. They helped to wear each other's (choleric) corners off! Mary even got over having

61

"opposititis" at home where she had once been a real problem.

These are only a few illustrations but the teacher hopes
they have given some idea of what a Rudolf Steiner kindergarten tries to bring to its tiny pupils.

After a year or two, through close, daily rhythmic activity
together, the children have learned the right kind of spontaneity, how to work in a group, and some measure of self-control. They are now ready to begin to learn and to use their
memories—in the First Grade—which has been their mecca
for some time.

(1941)   Alice Smith Jansen

On the Moral Education of
Younger Children*

When we attempt to speak on moral education, we feel
that this may not be done lightly but that our thoughts must
be deeply rooted. We even have a sense of strong discomfi-
ture when we speak on such a theme; a lifetime is insufficient
for acquiring knowledge of the human being, upon which
alone morality can be founded.

We realize that it is not sufficient to follow in the steps of
the natural sciences only. Knowledge of the body alone is not
enough. In order to be able to work in a way which is morally
fruitful, knowledge of the soul-spiritual being of man is
necessary, and we feel that we stand only at the beginning of
true research in this realm.

A further difficulty consists in our being unable to have
any influence on an individual human being so long as we

* Translated by Helen S. Belsterli from the bi-monthly magazine
  Erziehungskunst published by the teachers of the Waldorf School, Stuttgart,
  1935.

do not understand how physical body and soul-spiritual affect each other. Nothing can happen to or within man without body, soul and spirit being affected. It is not enough to know how to rear a healthy child and then to believe that we can inculcate into his healthy organism what we consider psychologically and spiritually suitable.

There is no such thing as physical science on the one hand and ethics on the other and we cannot consider what is within apart from what is without, the body separate from the soul. This may only be done in the case of someone who has died, but then we only have a corpse before us. We must learn to understand man as a working unit of body, soul and spirit, as Goethe felt it to be when he said: "Naught is within, naught is without. For what is within, that is without."

Our present-day culture has sundered the religious and moral element in man from the physical and natural one, and we must now learn to comprehend them as a working unity once more. We must learn to see man as a complete human being by seeing the interplay of both these members of his being. This is also the goal which is striven for in the educational system of the Waldorf school.

There is another point that I would like to place before you. A person as he stands before us, closed off within his skin, is not simply a spatial being. Rudolf Steiner has taught us to look upon him as a "time being" as well. The picture of a plant rises before me as it progresses in time through the various stages of development. First comes the seed, then the seed leaves; then the leaf, the green calyx, finally the blossom's petals. One after the other we experience the metamorphoses of the plant—its continual transformation. The human being as a time organism goes through such continual changes also, for his bodily, soul and spirit faculties are not all present at the same time but unfold gradually in more or less apparent rhythms. We know the more obvious rhythms as, for instance, in the change of teeth and puberty.

The question now arises for the teacher: "What special physical, soul and spirit relationships does childhood present, and how must my educational measures be constituted so that my efforts within these relationships will further and quicken the child—not injure and weaken him?"

Such questions awaken a deeper feeling of conscience and a greater sense of responsibility in the educator. He learns to pay a much closer attention to the finer measures of education, much more so than he had perhaps done before, and he learns to reckon with far-reaching effects.

It often happens that parents see something naughty in a child. Then they are apt to resort to some kind of universal remedy, perhaps in the very next moment, in order to eliminate the misbehavior as rapidly as possible. But in this way the naughtiness is only suppressed, because they have not the patience to hold a waiting attitude toward the child, and the remedy is not based on insight into the child's nature. In fact the naughtiness may be repeated again and again, but if, out of the knowledge of the child's nature, one is confident of having found the right thing for him, then the healing effect will gradually show itself. In questions regarding the education of children, one is always led back to a consideration of the adult, for education is in the most eminent sense self-education. Uneducated persons cannot educate, and there are more such than we often believe. Selflessness and self-dedication are basic necessities for the educator. More and more the realization grows upon us that morality cannot be taught, it must be given ground from which to grow. To issue orders is of no value, not even in the subtler manner in which we try to influence the other human being forcibly by the example of our own ethical character—when children are to be made into what we would like to have them become. A person can only be moral when, as a free being, he creates morality from out his innermost nature. This he cannot do in his early childhood; what is to develop itself freely as morality after his fourteenth year must be planted in him like a seed between his first and seventh years. The moral freedom or non-freedom of a human being is planted in him seed-like between his first and seventh years.

Let us consider the development of the infant. Before birth it rests in the womb of the mother whose body is a protective sheath. This is also the periphery from which influences radiate toward the child as toward a center. All that happens to the mother is imparted to the child's body; it is exposed to the influences emanating from the mother. The question is often asked: Is there a pre-natal education? To this one can only answer: Yes, there is one. It is the absolute and strictest education of the mother's own self through herself. No direct educational influence can be brought to bear on the child in the mother's womb.

The knowledge of how the child is so thoroughly protected in the body of the mother before birth gives us a good clue as to how he will find his way after birth into the body of the family. Just as the mother had to care for him when he was still within her body, so now the family must take care to see that the child's surroundings are sound. Just as good light and color are part and parcel of healthy eyesight, so the sound moral development of the child requires that a healthy moral life surround him. Not the moral phrases of the adults, but their moral actions are what count, and the child takes these in with his whole being. We might even say that he gulps them, for he takes his surroundings into himself as deeply as we do when we breathe in the outer air and drive it into the very depths of our body, making it into our inner world.

Of immense importance for the forming of the child's body is the kind of moral life which surrounds him. Never again in later life does such a surrender to his environment occur, not even through love. Even the unspoken thoughts of the persons around him affect the child. He senses whether the thoughts of those about him move more slowly or more quickly. He feels his father's energy and life-courage, his mother's kindness and love as active forces. The moral sensitivity of his surroundings forms his moral interests and also shapes his organism harmoniously. Weariness of life, withdrawal from life, weaken the moral forces of the child for his whole future, unless an educator later on realizes this and takes it in hand. Even his organism is affected inharmoniously by such qualities.

Children are tremendously healthy. Predispositions to illness are laid in them through the behavior of the human beings around them. Dishonest people, hypocrites for instance, who set up laws which they themselves do not observe, injure the child. Untruthfulness injures him, even his physical organism, and this can cause a tendency toward disturbances of the metabolic system later in life. Whence these disturbances come is often unknown by then, because we are not accustomed to pay attention to such connections.

If it is desired that a child acquire a certain attribute, this is dependent upon its being "done" in the child's surroundings. He does not acquire the feeling of gratitude from being taught to say *thank you* and to bow or curtsy. He learns gratitude when the adults with whom he lives are able to say *thank you* out of a sincerely experienced feeling of gratefulness, for instance, towards servants. In this respect much is wanting. By reason of having observed and imitated gratitude, the child will learn later on not to accept as a matter of course what others do for him.

All that goes on around the child in the way of foolish or sensible actions affects his organs in a health-promoting or injurious manner. From the first to the seventh year his organism develops forms and tendencies which it then retains for his whole lifetime. Foolish actions affect the child's brain and can even shape it so that later on it also can give out only foolish thoughts. The child becomes dull.

The father says: "Where does he get it from? Certainly not from me!" The mother says: "Nor from me!" They do not ask themselves whether their actions, observed by the child, may not have aided in bringing about this state.

Many parents, with good intentions toward their children, give them mechanical toys. By doing so they mechanize the child's brain and suppress something which he needs urgently. They paralyze his imagination, his creative spiritual forces.

We aid him to develop healthy imaginative forces by giving the child incomplete toys. When playing railway, for instance, simply let him use tables and chairs even though it cause disorder, for this is better than the perfect products of the latest toy-manufacturing technology.

The emotions of adults exercise a very strong influence upon children. Let us suppose that there is a rift between the parents giving rise to quarrels and scoldings. The child may be sitting in the corner playing, apparently not listening. He nevertheless takes in his parents' emotions with his whole being. His breathing grows faster or slower, his circulation quicker or more halting. The dread he feels makes his lips dry and a bitter taste on his tongue. In such a way very, very much is done in regard to his moral upbringing, towards making or unmaking the moral education of a child; the adults do not hold themselves responsible for it.

Let attention be called to another phenomenon. According to the insight of Rudolf Steiner there occurs, when the child is being born, a union of something coming, one can say, from heaven, from the spiritual world, with something coming from the earth. The eternal being of the child, its "ego", is given a body by the parents; but the meeting of these two is not always a happy one. A comparison may help us here. We may have a suit that fits perfectly or does not fit well, it pinches here or there, we slip into it in this way or that and it always causes a feeling of discomfort. The eternal being of a child may feel such discomfort in regard to its body. Sometimes the union takes place without friction, then the children are well-balanced and do not cry much. Other children behave badly and cry a lot. But we cease to be angered when we comprehend that there is a struggle, a resistance against taking possession of the body, of fitting into it. And this struggle may last a long time. As a rule strong natures have to undergo this struggle, they have more difficulty than weaker ones. It is harder for them to lay hold of or form their body. Children's diseases are also connected with the difficulties that the human ego experiences in connection with a body that does not yet fit it. These difficulties first express themselves through the soul in whining and naughty behavior. The child has everything he needs in the way of food and play and he is not content. He is scolded as ungrateful, simply because we do not understand him. These difficulties then express themselves more strongly, even physically, in children's diseases.*

For the moral education of the child everything is important that goes on around him while he is learning to *walk, talk and think*. With his kicking, the child is preparing himself to learn to speak. From orderly speech orderly thinking is developed and this is the proper sequence in the development of the child. What does it mean for a child's life that he learns to walk, talk and think? It signifies the first rising-up of humanity towards humanity, the first overcoming of animality. It means conquering necessity, the first act of freedom. A child raises his countenance to heaven, frees his front limbs from the earth, moving them freely, and thus makes the first bodily step toward becoming a human being.

In learning to walk the child orientates himself in space and finds his relationship to the world. It is a mistaken kind of ambition to want to hasten this learning. Such misguided action on the part of the grownups may in later life give rise to a disposition towards gout and rheumatism. We wonder then where the diseases come from. Perhaps an explanation could be found by looking deeper into the underlying relationships.

When we observe the way in which a child walks we can see something of his childish character. How he places his feet, bends his knee, uses his little fingers, all this can serve us as a clue to his character as it will reveal itself in the future.

* See Dr. zur Linden's article in this volume.

In learning to speak the child enters into connection with the spirit of his people, and this learning to speak should proceed correctly; it is important for his moral development. Adults should see to it that truthfulness reigns in the child's surroundings, and not show a lack of it by imitating the babblings of the child. Only after the child has learned to speak properly can he learn to think properly.

Through thinking he becomes a part of common humanity. He acquires what is common to all men. For the sake of his future moral development we ourselves should avoid being confused, for all inconsistency in our thinking injures the child. For instance, one should not give an order and then countermand it after a short while. If the adult educator can not avoid confusion in his thinking, there is created in the child the possibility of future nervousness, and a lack of self-control.

If the child has had a proper upbringing between the first and seventh years he will develop a strong will, and this will is the portal through which he takes into himself the external world.

If at this age the child has the right model to imitate, then he will at the same time receive the best moral education, because at this time there lives in him the unconscious but strong belief that *the world is good and is worthy of imitation.*

At the age of six or seven the child starts going to school. The teacher does not find him an unwritten page, for he brings with him influences from his surroundings, influences which have been stamped into him like the impressions of a seal. Teachers should endeavor to sharpen their eyes for such seal-impressions and then be able to recognize the ethical love that surrounded the child, or even the lack of warmth and love that have affected him and brought about an inharmonious development. They can trace, for example, in the frequent paleness of a child at school, the weariness of life which has made its impression upon him at home. Here the teacher can help, not by ridding the child of such impressions, which turn into traits of character, but by transforming them. The child's fear may be changed into self-possession and discernment. The opportunity may be offered him to transform fearfulness into courage and strength of judgment. This the teacher can emphasize. It is just between the seventh and fourteenth year that there is as yet nothing in the child that cannot be transformed into good. Rudolf Steiner has pointed this out again and again. The belief in the child's ability to change should become a permanent attitude of mind on the part of parents and teachers.

At this age a child should be neither judged nor condemned. Jean Paul once said: "Furthermore let it become a law, that every force is holy. No force is to be weakened, but over against it let another be awakened; thus, for instance, an over-tender, loving soul is not to be hardened, but the power of honor and clarity in it strengthened. In this way a bold character is not to be made fearful but lovingly and judiciously formed."* Just as the child between the first and seventh year took in his surroundings, so he now listens to the world of authority resounding near him. A great deal of veneration and respect appears within the child at this time between the seventh and fourteenth years. These forces must be preserved in him and become effective in his moral education, for nothing is attained at this stage of development by the categorical imperative and by simply giving orders. On the other hand moral judgment founded on feeling is to be cultivated. It is important that everything which the teacher has to relate to the children be related with an undertone of feeling. Their sympathies and antipathies should be engaged in what he presents. Sympathy for what is moral and antipathy for what is immoral will in this way be awakened in the children by the teacher.

Thus in teaching history he will tell them of exemplary men and women. He will awaken in the children sympathy

* Jean Paul Richter, 1763-1825, novelist and humorist in the period of German Romanticism.

for good and antipathy for bad qualities by describing them in a vivid way. If the teacher notices an undesirable characteristic in a child, he will do well not to attack this peculiarity directly. He will do better to tell the child a story in which this quality plays a corresponding role and he will then wait and see what the child makes of it. He does not exhort, but presents the moral quality by means of a picture. For example, he allows animals with the most varied characteristics to speak and act before the child's imagination, and in this way works, through the pictures, upon his moral feeling.

If a young choleric, for instance, commits some folly in an access of rage, he will, for the moment, only keep him from doing any damage. Not till the next day perhaps will the teacher take him aside, let him relate what took place and talk it over with him. Now that his emotions have died down he can face himself quietly. Moral education during the school period must be based on truthfulness. For this reason the educator must learn to be willing to allow the child to live out his true nature beside him and before his very eyes. If by using severity we repress all that the child would otherwise live out, we force him to commit all kinds of nonsense behind our backs.

About the ninth and tenth year an important moment arrives in the child's life. He becomes more conscious, more thoughtful, more personal. Inwardly he questions the teacher, he questions life: "Is your authority really the right one to present the world to me? Can I go on having confidence in you?" An inner restlessness disturbs the child until he receives an answer to this question, until the teacher, either directly or indirectly, says to him: "I can tell you still more about the world, things more beautiful than you have learned from me so far." If he is satisfied in his often unspoken questioning, if he can feel confidence, then his moral character will also grow stronger and more settled. Rudolf Steiner has often pointed out that there are old people who have a beneficent effect on us. Even without their speaking to us we feel blessed in being with them. They shed a blessing about them. If we look into the fact more closely, we find that such persons can bless because as children they have had the good fortune to be able to look up with reverence to an authority whom they venerated. Hands that learn to fold in prayer when young can dispense blessings in old age.

Jean Paul says: "Of what does warmth consist for the little human babe? Joyfulness! I can endure a sad man, but not a sad child; no matter into what morass the former has sunk, he can raise his eyes either to the realm of reason or to that of hope; but the little child becomes altogether enveloped and crushed by one poisonous, black drop of the Present."

Just as important as the sun is for the plant seed, so is cheerful serenity the true happiness for the development of children. Cheerfulness, truthfulness, genuine love, form the truly nourishing soil from which the child's moral character can grow.

And something else. The child should be guarded from experiencing too early a feeling of guilt. We should endeavor, just as long as possible, to preserve the child's feeling of innocence. All the more does one assure the development of the moral force which has to prove itself later in life.

What the child is to take in between the seventh and fourteenth year he can only take in in an artistic way through his feelings, just as between the first and seventh year he takes in the world through his will. By this means he acquires a soul quality, namely gratefulness. Now in these later years love should find its proper unfolding in the child.

My intention was not to impart the details of a moral education, but to indicate the inner attitude out of which alone moral education can be achieved. This must first be developed in ourselves if we wish to be able to educate.

In closing let me quote some words by Therese Schroer* which speak of this attitude and which may accompany us. Looking upon her children whom she had brought up with

---

* Mother of Rudolf Steiner's literature professor at the Vienna Institute of Technology; she wrote a book to help mothers educate their children.

great patience and with unbounded love and wisdom, she says: "Youth has transition periods when it needs forbearance and gentle guidance, . . . children may not be pressed and pushed through the portal from one life-period into the next. In watching over them we must give them as guiding companions quiet, love and self-abnegation. Do we believe ourselves exhausted, ready to sink down in complete weariness of heart? Then let us say to ourselves: 'With God's help it may be better tomorrow.' And frequently it is so. Then comes and hour, a day, and our daughter, our son has cast off the chrysalis and the soul spreads its wings towards us."

(1947)   Christoph Boy

Look at a child from behind . . . some walk by planting the whole foot on the ground, others trip along on their toes; there can be every kind of differentiation between these two extremes. Yes indeed, to educate a child one must know precisely how he or she walks.

Rudolf Steiner
Kingdom of Childhood

Adventures in the Park

There could not be a better playground for a city school than a park. The Rudolf Steiner School in New York City has the good fortune to be only a half block away from Central Park; the kindergarten children and I could roam around it in all directions. We knew it well and loved it. In all sorts of weather, cold or hot, sunny or windy, we went to the park (except on rainy days) and we had our favorite spots. One of them was "our big rock."

One day a little boy told me his father had read him the story of Moby Dick. It must have been a children's version—but I thought, Those fathers! can't they wait until the time is right? But the genius of childhood takes care of many things, and so it happened that most of our little boys turned into Captain Ahab and in the park were forever searching for Moby Dick. Our big rock turned into a whaler, manned by all those Captain Ahabs. Once as I was sitting on a bench below the rock, watching the rest of my little flock playing about me, an urgent call came down, "Come up! Come up! We saw Moby Dick out there!" I called up to them, "I have such a comfortable little boat: couldn't you make it safe for me?" I can still see the heavy coils of rope with which they fastened my boat by an intricate process to their larger one. I was declared safe, and they climbed back to continue their search.

There was another rock, long and low, just like a boat, out in the meadow. Several children were playing there when a little fellow ran excitedly towards me, yelling, "Did you know Peter almost got drowned?" "Oh no!" I said, "You didn't go out into those deep, dangerous waters where the whirlpools are?" "Don't worry," he said, in a fatherly way. "We saved him! We threw him a life preserver."

At the school fair a mother and father had bought their little son a wooden sword, almost as big as he was and heavy. He brought it to school, of course, and begged me to let him take it to the park. "No," I said, "It's much too heavy and you will want me to carry it." "I will carry it," he assured me. "I will!" I decided to take a chance. When we had crossed the street and entered the park, up went the sword. He had turned into King Arthur with Excalibur, and in his wake followed all the Knights of the Round Table. This game lasted not only for days and days but for weeks.

In the park at Easter time we met the Easter bunny, that is, we found the eggs he had left for us. I had to tell the children how many each could take, for there were quick children who would have gathered them all; the slower ones would not have had any. As we approached our big rock, around which the eggs were hidden, a hush fell over the children. Who knows? The Easter bunny might still be near! One of the little boys, with lower lip protruding, said, "My parents don't believe in that stuff." Then his face lighting up, he exclaimed, "But I do, I do."

We had favorite trees. One was a grandfather tree, a mighty sycamore. It took six children pressed flat against its trunk and holding hands to give it a good hug. There was a climbing tree: one had to stretch a bit to reach the lowest branches, but the higher ones were arranged in easy steps like a circular stairway. Some of the children were up like squirrels to the top of the tree in no time at all; there were others who hung on the lowest branches like bags filled with water. Whenever one of the slow, heavy ones reached the top, everyone rejoiced loudly.

Once in the spring, we passed a tiny tree in full bloom. A little boy pointed it out to me: "Look! a little girl tree!" And so it was, all dressed in pink.

We discovered two locust trees close together, which in the fall dropped an abundance of beans. We brought shopping bags to collect them and on a rainy day, we peeled them. The kernels are hard, brown and polished. Our school secretary came into the room and asked, "Whatever are you going to do with all those beans?" Why, they can be stirred in little pots and cooked, they can be dropped into little boxes and cans, they can be weighed or put into equal piles, they can

75

be served in the doll corner as a meal—just to hold them in your hand is fun !

On a glorious day in May we went to our little valley. It has steep sides and a tiny brook flowing through it. If it ever could receive some care, it would be a small paradise,—but we liked it as it was. We could float small pieces of wood in the water, build bridges and dams, jump across the little stream and slip and get our shoes wet, throw pebbles into the water. Two of my girls approached and asked, "Could you be our mother?" "Of course, I will be your mother," I said. "Can we go to the woods, Mother?" they inquired. "Yes," I said, "You can go to the woods but don't go too near the witch's house and if you see the wolf, don't talk to him." And off they went. Two other little girls had been listening and now they too wanted to know whether I would be their mother. "Of course, I will be your mother, too." "Please say the same thing to us," they begged. So I said the same thing all over again: "You can go to the woods but don't go too near the witch's house and if you see the wolf, don't talk to him."

When it was time to go "home", we passed a long azalea hedge in full, flaming bloom. The sky was blue with spring clouds. "Mother, where are we going?" the little girls wanted to know. "We are going back to our castle and we will eat from our golden plates and drink from our golden cups." We walked a little above the earth.

(1976)   Lona Koch

Eurythmy Lessons for Children of
Three to Seven*

Through our modern life we soon lose what in our childhood was still a fresh and natural union with the original forces of the sounds of speech. For through our everyday conversation, which pays service to necessities only, these sounds are robbed of their magic; they become profane and lifeless for us. Daily our gaze is directed to the phrases of advertisements and the names of merchandise, and in these the combinations of sounds have, in the truest sense, no longer anything in common with the present content or value of the words. The roar of the technical world presses in upon our ears, drowning out the sounds of nature and making us unreceptive to them.

If, however, children have had eurythmy lessons over a longer period of time, speech will never be something lifeless for them. They will always keep and carry in their consciousness a sense and appreciation of the nature of word sounds.

In such eurythmy lessons everything must be brought to the three to seven year old children in the form of pictures. These they must be able to imitate. This is in keeping with the capacities of their age. The more one can give the children something beautiful and genuine as an example and an ideal, the easier it is to keep alive for them their capacity for wonder and amazement.

For a child, the vowel O is synonymous with the picture of an "open rose", or perhaps of "holding a golden bowl". As of their own accord, when these words are spoken, their arms close in a loving, rounded O. The vowel A (pronounced as in late), on the other hand, forms itself out of the picture of a "grated gate" or a "gay little shoe-maker nailing away", and their arms cross or strike each other firmly. When they look up to see how "far the stars are", their arms open

* Translated from *Das Goetheanum*, September 12, 1948, by Christy Barnes.

wonderingly into the wide angle of the broad A (Ah). In E they stretch and shine out—"See! like a sunbeam reaching out to the steep snow peaks". With the whole power of their beings children can give expression to the feeling of love, of holding themselves firm, of wonder, and of bright out-going. (These are naturally only some of the simplest examples.)

Through the consonants the children are led into the weavings of nature They imitate the W, for example, in the wind that whistles over wood and wilderness, or they wander winding ways to where warm waves are washing. In B they hold protectingly in their arms a baby, a bundle or a bird. In R the rain runs and rushes till the rivers roar. Lightly the flowers flutter and jingle their little bells, blow and blossom with L. In such pictures of nature the consonants become alive for the children. Nature weaves and wells, showers and shines, ripples and rumbles all about them when one teaches them to listen, to pay attention to the tiniest, finest things around them. Their motions are identical with these processes; the children are themselves wind and wave.

If we seek out the right images, we can prevent children from walking through nature unheeding. We can awaken in them a love for things which otherwise they would perhaps pass by. How often a child tells how he has seen a snail which slowly, very slowly stretched out its feelers, or that he found a bird's nest—things which through their sounds we had lived with during the last lesson.

In this way the right kind of imitation grows into a force for the children, a force against becoming unfeeling and dulled.

Some Words about the Forming of a Lesson

These pictures, which are brought to the children during the lesson, must now be formed into a unified structure. From the beginning to the end of a lesson the children must be *carried along* and *led through* all that happens

We should never say, "Now we will do this", but from the very beginning one train of events must be led over into the next in a significant way so that a rounded whole is the result. One can base the course of the lesson upon a certain rhythm for a while, for instance on the iambic (short, long), or on the anapaest (short, short, long), and let these rhythms come to the fore again and again in the most varied activities: in beating time or clapping, in walking, knocking, chopping, etc. Forms, staff exercises, poems, verses, ring-games can also be brought into the procession of events without, however, breaking into their on-flowing progress! If one does not succeed thus in carrying the children along and leading them on, one will scarcely be able to keep them together or to interest them. During the jumps in thought which would then occur from time to time, they would surely run away and have to be brought back once more with considerable effort. Therefore a very exact preparation must precede the lessons and nevertheless one must remain quite open and flexible. From beginning to end one must take part in everything with the children in order to give them at each moment a beautiful example to imitate. And so each child, no matter how different he may be from the others, partakes of the lesson equally and is alike carried along by each gesture.

Whoever teaches children for any length of time will soon have the experience that the same thing must be repeated at least four times, each time a little left out and something new brought in in its place. In this way the children can fully live into and with an experience.

For they can get great joy from already knowing what is going to happen. They want to be able to link onto what happened in the last lesson. They often come with the question, "Are we going to visit the dwarfs and giants again today?" And they expect "Yes" for an answer.

The best starting point for teaching lies in the seasons and their festivals.

In autumn it is the storms that rattle the trees till the apples and leaves fall to the ground; it is the wind that rustles the bushes; it is the dwarfs and giants at work in the woods. In winter the snowflakes fly through the air and cover up the earth. Then Mary rocks her Child, and to her come wandering the proud kings and merry shepherds; the angels come flying. In spring we hunt the early wild flowers in the moss, stretch ourselves in the sun. There a butterfly flutters by and the birds are singing. In summer we wander with the ducks to the lake, up the mountains to the cows.

So we find an inexhaustible wealth of material when we awaken in ourselves the *imagination* without which it would be altogether impossible to teach children. Then, just as Rudolf Steiner wished we need *explain nothing* to the children.

Some Nodal Points from Teaching Experience

It is good always to do the same exercises at the beginning of the lesson, for instance, "Where is my head?" "Right here!" "Where are my legs?" "There they are!" in order that the children come into relation with their bodies and their limbs rightly, and stand firmly on the ground. The same is true for the close of the lesson, for instance an earnest verse ("See the bright sun's shining power!" for example). For the children should never run hastily out of the lesson, Rudolf Steiner once told a eurythmist. One can let them stand quietly for a moment, listening inwardly once more to what they have just experienced and so they carry something beautiful with them out of the lesson.

One should also mention that children love something ceremoniously beautiful, and are respectfully, even reverently attentive, but that one must never let this mood of devotion last too long, for it is not in keeping with their years. Therefore a great aid to the teacher is the *harmonious interchange of opposites*. One can let loud and soft, earnest and joyful, large and little, release one another. If, for instance, the giants were large and loud and walked with great, heavy strides, the dwarfs are tiny, light, and trip with quick little steps. If the kings march with measured and ceremonious tread, then the shepherds run merrily. Thus the tension of the children is never overstrained, but is always released and led over into its opposite which they can then always *take up freshly*. One must sense from the children's own souls when "enough" has come.

Such an interchange can be brought about even within a poem or a song. If after a while one suddenly calls "Shhhh!" softly, making the quieting S in eurythmy and at the same time all draw closer together, the children will immediately do the poem with you in a mood suggestive of mystery, growing more inward and delicate in their gestures. One must then grasp this moment of listening and lead it over into the further courses of the lesson. The children can be brought to attention by the quieting influence of the S. One need not shout, "Quiet now!" but only make *the eurythmy gesture for the sound S*.

All this Rudolf Steiner wished to have accompanied by music. For a musician this is no simple task, for he must improvise freely, fill each passing moment and accompany the course of events. In this way the change from loud to soft can be brought out, and the children's feet find a particular rhythm more easily. If one has no pianist and no instrument, one can help oneself with singing.

One must hear in the nature of the child himself what is needed in order to form a lesson. To be thoroughly prepared and yet take hold of each situation freely are necessities, as we said before. But spread out over all teaching like a bright shimmering must lie a joy which unites pupils and teacher. Imagination and joy together are surely the best pre-requisites for the instruction of children.

The Necessity for Children's Eurythmy

We mentioned in the beginning that through our modern life our original connection with word sounds has been lost. It is evident that most of the children who have come to us from war-torn countries have never known beautiful speech. Again and again ten-year-old children have begged to take part in the lessons with the little ones as though they wanted to make up for what they had not experienced. Where had they ever heard fairy tales or poems, or even beautiful sounds? At first they could only slowly bring to expression through their movements their love for some other thing or being, and win back a child's capacity for wondering, loving and being able to enjoy himself.

A child must be allowed to bring to expression the stirring of beauty in his soul if he is to be capable later in life of looking into the surrounding world with certainty, and grasping each situation consciously. To nurture this and give to children what is not otherwise often at hand is made possible today through the eurythmy Rudolf Steiner has given us, and to do this is urgently necessary.

(1949)   Margarethe Buehler

The Inner Meaning of Children's Diseases: Measles

Let me start with a comparison. A man moves into a house that he has inherited from his parents. He likes it fairly well, but in its present state it doesn't quite suit him. It seems to be arranged according to his parents' tastes and habits, and he is not merely their son but also an individual with his own ideas, plans and work. Therefore he starts to renovate the house completely; he tears down and builds up, indoors and out, until—in six or seven years' time—he has changed everything in accordance with *his* needs, *his* preferences, *his* particular personality.

What an adult human being carries out in this way in full consciousness, our ego—our inner spiritual kernel—carries out in our first seven years, certainly without a knowledge of its aims but nevertheless with the greatest intensity, order and wisdom. In the depths of our spiritual nature there is a vast treasure of hidden wisdom, which every newborn child brings with him.

With his first breath, the spiritual nature of the child, his ego, "moves into" the body inherited from his parents. He begins to remodel his "house", according to the needs of his personality, and in the course of the first six or seven years of life, he will have transformed all the material of his body. At the end of this time he even throws out his baby teeth, as if he wants us to be aware that a complete transformation has taken place. By this time the child's body has been built over in its entirety, down to the last body cell, transmuted indeed; now it corresponds to the individuality and uniqueness of this particular ego.

The fact that the body of every seven-year-old child stands on the earth as a single, unique creation—into the structure of every hair, into the very lines on every finger—shows that the spirit which is impressing itself so individually upon the bodily material cannot be a product of heredity, cannot be the end-result of a purely physical line of evolution: it can only be understood as an active spirit-seed with its own specific form—this spirit-seed which we call the ego.

But each individual ego is not only filled with new impulses, new ideas, new intentions, but is driven by a tremendous, uncontrollable will to live. This is the origin of the extraordinary achievements the ego has to bring about every day, every hour, indeed every minute, through an entire lifetime—and at no time in such variety and intensity as during the years of early childhood.

The child's ego has more and more to become "head of the household", master of its body, until it has learned to control all its functions—from grasping, sitting, standing, speaking, orientating itself in space, to thinking, feeling and many other faculties. It must take charge of an ordered interplay of its inner organs, a task truly immeasurable in scope. Besides bodily growth and development already mentioned, one must point to other life processes: health, illness, recovery, regeneration.

Take measles as an example. Of the authentic children's diseases with the common symptom, a red skin eruption: measles, scarlet fever and German measles, the inner meaning is especially clear. Someone has discovered a name for it: "a help-towards-life". It describes the situation perfectly.

I once had to treat a little pair of identical twins who had measles. One of them had a severe onset of the illness with high fever, while the little sister's symptoms were quite mild. When the illness had run its course, the twin who had been so severely ill recovered remarkably well; she was obviously impelled to greater physical health and inner steadiness. The little sister, however, had afterward to struggle for a long time in her bodily development and showed a lack of harmony. Thus the same contagious disease can take its course in identical twins with quite different intensity and can have correspondingly different effects. And thus the "help-towards-life" of the illness was fully active only in one case. The example also shows that a disease is not something foreign, breaking in from the outside to penetrate a human being, nor is it something carried into a healthy person by some germ or other: otherwise there could not be so many different courses of the disease and so many outcomes. The illness is always latent in the person, and the germ only gives the last thrust towards the onset.

Almost all children need measles for their healthy development, and so their organism is prepared for the disease. For this reason almost every exposure leads to the illness. A person who has not been "measled through" is hard to find. Even the slightest exposure to an acute case, especially in the days just preceding the skin eruption, leads after ten or eleven days to a catarrhal condition that starts this new case, the skin eruption following then three or four days later. We can recognize the nature of measles from the picture the course of the disease paints on the child's skin. Accompanying a quickly rising fever, the skin of the face becomes bloated so that the features are washed out, become indefinite. The mucous membranes of eyes, nose, throat, larynx, and trachea also show inflamed swellings and have mucous discharge. Starting behind the ears, a rash of large red spots spreads over the head and then over the entire body, including even the inner mucous membranes. Soon the child cannot tolerate the light, there is a cold, conjunctivitis, and catarrh of the air passages. In rare cases there is even an increase in the pressure of the cerebro-spinal fluid, causing fainting spells or convulsions. Tiny white specks, like sprinkled powder, appearing on the mucous membrane inside the cheeks, are the infallible symptom that enables the doctor to diagnose the illness as measles; often it is not easy to diagnose, as compared for instance with German measles.

There is apparent in all these phenomena a kind of turmoil, a kind of rebellion, in the fluid organism of the child—whose body consists, after all, of 70% water. With measles an abnormal amount of fluid pushes into the skin of the face and into the mucous membranes of the air passages. Fever, and the fact that it is often quite high, points directly to the activity of the ego. The ego has obviously induced all this revolt. After three or four days the rash begins to pale, the facial swellings go down, the inflammation and itching of the mucous membranes subside, cough and cold disappear, and the child quickly recovers. But there are also cases with severe, stubborn cough and the feeling of being quite ill.

In the weeks that follow, an observant person can notice not only a gratifying balancing and adjusting of the child's nature that has overcome a few bad habits, but also often striking changes in the features of the face. Parents report with astonishment that a former likeness to father or mother has vanished; the child has found himself through the illness, even as far as his facial features. The whole process is a particularly vivid example of the transformation of the "body-model" spoken of so often, which the human ego has to accomplish during childhood. Measles gives the child's ego the opportunity to penetrate his inherited formative forces, and so to transform his inherited tendencies that he can thereby obtain the individual form that is right for him.

—Wilhelm zur Linden, M.D.
(*Translated by Gladys Hahn*)

Importance of Fairy Tales in a Rudolf Steiner School

Fairy tales form the foundation for the teaching in the kindergarten, first and second grades of a Rudolf Steiner school. The folk fairy tales of various nations and of ancient times, such as the Grimms collected, are considered as basic education. Out of them grow the other subjects—painting, drawing, writing, counting, eurythmy, as taught in the elementary grades.

We are well aware that this is a departure from present-day practice, for in our modern times fairy tales have come to be lightly regarded. The questions are often asked: why should fairy stories be told at all? Do they not develop in our children a sense of the impractical, of idle fantasy? Some people do tell fairy stories to young children, but they regard them only as poetic entertainment, as a reward for good behavior or a means of quieting at bed-time.

The teachers in a Rudolf Steiner school have an entirely different attitude toward this fairy lore. Their feeling about it and understanding of it is inspired by Rudolf Steiner's research into the cosmic order, which has made possible a new observation of children. Anyone who watches a child in the midst of unaffected play sees that he is building a world for himself that is like a paradise. Play is a sort of dream, and the dreaming is a manifestation of an artistic union with the world around the child.

Naturally, as a human being, a child has his own individuality. But he must leave this dream state before he can gradually awaken himself to his own selfhood. This inner self is hidden behind many screens, or shell-like layers, as is suggested by the seven mountains enclosing Snowwhite's dwelling place.

While the soul of the child plays in this dreaming-artistic state he meets no temptations or dangers. Adults with the right spiritual understanding know that, for the child, the whole world seems bewitched and enchanted. But at the moment when his soul begins to awaken to his inner consciousness, he loses his paradise. Then a new period begins—a period of struggle with those adversaries that hinder the discovery of his own personality. The child longs to discover his own selfhood. And the telling of fairy stories meets this longing as nothing else can do. It helps him to unfold to the realities of the world about him, gently, without shock.

In most fairy stories we find a prince and princess as the central figures. Do we not see in them the more masculine element of the "ego" and the more feminine element of the soul? Remember in what a variety of ways the bewitched prince or enchanted princess is finally set free. The ultimate marriage pictures the conscious union of the two (soul and "ego") after many trials. It is the happy discovery of the awakened human self—at last freed from its enchantment.

From this point of view let us look at "The Frog Prince," one of the well-known Grimms' tales. Once upon a time (which means it can happen any day to anybody) there was a princess, the youngest daughter of an old king. (The old king represents the ancient state of man, the past which offers no glimpse of the future.) The princess played every day with a golden ball. (This symbolizes the wonderful paradise in which the true game of childhood is always played.) One day the ball did not drop back into the hand of the princess but fell to the ground and rolled down the well.

At once an ugly frog appeared and asked the princess why she was crying.

"I can fetch your ball," said the frog, "but if I do, what will you give me?" It is made plain that he did not want pearls or gold or even a golden crown; he wished only to participate in the personality of the little princess. This is very significant. "Let me sit at your table," he said, "eat out of your plate, drink from your cup and sleep in your bed." The princess promised all this, took her ball and joyously ran off with it.

Next day when the king's family sat at dinner, the frog appeared at the castle and called out, "Youngest daughter of the king, you must let me in." The princess did not want to do it but when the old king heard what had happened he said, "What you have promised you must perform." So the princess opened the door and the frog hopped in. He sat at her table and ate and drank. When the princess could no longer stand the sight of the ugly frog, she flung him with all her might against the wall. But it was not the frog which picked himself up. A handsome prince stood there before her, free of his bewitchment. And so the prince and the princess were married and lived happily ever after.

In the art and fantasy of these old fairy tales is hidden a deep wisdom which has the power to awaken children from the sleep of ordinary earthly life. But only if the teller is able to believe in the reality of such stories will they have the desired effect. According to the principles of biogenetic law, children pass briefly through all stages of mankind's evolution. Fairy tales have their origin in the period of humanity's own childhood, those far-distant times when people lived in a naive, dreamlike state of soul before the unfolding of intellectual capacity. Fairy tales, then, lead the child's soul by the shortest and most direct way through these stages of human development. Unhappily, this is far from true of the usual modern books for children.

If we tell such stories in the right mood and believe in their higher content, they will inspire children to draw and paint, to recite and act, to write and count, to trust and think in the right way.

Forces of healing are also hidden in each fairy tale. As the child listens and remembers, he passes through fear and compassion and astonishment to a feeling of awe and devotion toward the invisible world. This may be considered the most important result of telling fairy tales. They stimulate the feeling that man is a being of development, of struggle, of metamorphosis, and that behind all the adverse forces of giants and dwarfs, witches and demons there lies the good world of the true genius of man.

Between the ages of four or five to eight or nine, the child plays in the meadows of paradise much as the princess in the Grimms' fairy tale. After that age the child must lose paradise in order to awaken. Such fairy tales provide the best nourishment for the child's soul during this period and give him the right help in awakening into earthly reality.

That we are able to think at all about these problems or to understand the importance of fairy tales is because Rudolf Steiner has given us a new feeling for education and for the child as a human being. His inexhaustible wisdom concerning the child's development led straight to the realm of the fairy tales. They inspire teachers themselves, more and more, as they learn to grasp their inner meaning. They reveal themselves differently to every individual teacher, for the truth contained in each one of them is neither one-sided nor narrow-minded. Fairy tales constitute a world of enormous space and varying perspective.

(1940)   Frederick Hiebel

III

THE FIRST FIVE GRADES

Morning Verse
Grades One through Four

The sun with loving light
Brightens for me the day;
The soul with spirit power
Gives strength unto my limbs.
In sunlight shining clear
I reverence, O God,
The source of human strength
Which Thou so graciously
Hast planted in my soul,
That I with all my heart
May love to work and learn.
From Thee come light and strength
To Thee stream love and thanks.

Rudolf Steiner

The Role of the Class Teacher
and Its Transformation

The founding of the Waldorf School in Stuttgart came from a social impulse, from the insight of Rudolf Steiner into social needs that were becoming clearly apparent in 1919. The school was intended to answer the question: how must people be educated in order to solve the social problems that present themselves in the 20th century—in order to solve them creatively, actively, constructively?

And so the school was founded as a school for *all* children. It was organized entirely on the basis of what is common to all human beings: the body-soul stages of development from childhood to adulthood which every person has to go through, regardless of background, sex, race, regardless also of intellectual capacity or practical talents and such occupational goals as result from these factors: thus, *co-education* in the most comprehensive sense, a class community based entirely on age, allowing no discrimination, no special groups, no failures!

We are often asked: does it really work? And it can actually happen that when we are confronted by a skeptical onlooker plus one's own uncertainty, we even ask ourselves the question: does it really work? isn't it really quite impossible? But truly it does work! Continuous observation over many years confirms this. Then what helps to make what appears impossible possible?

Two strong aids have often been described: the curriculum, planned according to the age-levels of the children, and the artistic method. A further aid (from among others) is the subject of the present discussion: the coming together of a class of individuals, a meeting by force of destiny.

At the center of this meeting stands first of all the class teacher, who receives the first-graders and who leads them through eight years of school. The children who are entrusted to him, the six- or seven-year-olds, are not yet a "class", even if they number thirty or more; they are just a crowd of children of the same age, who are congregating about the teacher as center of their new world. In no time at all the teacher has become father or mother to them, responsible for everything, dearly loved, and called upon as a matter of course in every emergency, whether there is a sorrow to be comforted or a shoe to be tied.

The importance of this for the lower grades is seldom questioned. But the fact that the teacher accompanies the children through eighth grade whenever possible is often looked upon dubiously, even by the teachers themselves, who have to shoulder this heavy task. And yet just here lies the blessing of such an arrangement.

On the one hand, through his long years of experience with them, the teacher acquires a deep knowledge of his individual children, their background, their potential, their learning-capacity and -tempo. He works painstakingly at forming the class in a social way, balancing, healing, giving every child a place, knowing the unique worth of each one and nurturing him accordingly.

At the same time, however, as teacher, he too is a learner. For even if he has carried another class through school before, it has been normally eight years since he concerned himself with the material he now has to use—time enough to practice forgetting and to become more demanding of himself. He will have to *learn anew* what he wishes now to *teach* to his pupils. And this learning process is different each time, not only because he is older, because the times have changed, science more advanced, but above all because now he has other children before him, with different questions and needs.

Although the children do not become fully conscious of it, still they do experience this effort to learn on the part of the teacher. The learning process becomes visible. It is precisely on those occasions in seventh or eighth grade when the pupil observes that the teacher is not just "pulling it out of his sleeve" with no effort at all but must first learn it himself—it is in those moments that the child has an intimate experience of the fact that man can learn, that learning need never stop, that it belongs to the noblest human faculties.

Thus the teacher *learns ahead* of his pupils, he learns for them and with them and leads them from year to year into new areas of learning. And when the richness of the various subjects becomes apparent, when along with English and mathematics the natural science courses appear, as well as history and geography and much more besides, then through their teacher the pupils become aware that one can learn everything, that the individual human being is the center of a whole world and, in knowing, can take a whole world into his grasp. The unity of the material which thus confronts the unity of the class becomes visible in the oneness of the learning teacher.

But this mood of soul is transformed when puberty sets in. Devotion to the class teacher gives place to joy in the variety of subject teachers. One's own capacity of criticism and judgment is gradually waking and wants to assert itself. The student must now learn to recreate the unity of a world that is thrusting itself upon him in such manifold ways. And the image he has unconsciously absorbed through the years is what gives him confidence in his own new task: the image of the learning teacher, who was able to unite in his single intelligence all the subjects that now approach the young person from this side and that, ever more demandingly, and that require to be mastered by him.

At this time, then, in the social framework of the school, what takes the place of the class teacher?—who takes over his functions? It is this that people find hard to accept today, for the answer is the class itself, the age-group class, one can also call it the class-by-destiny; the community of children, of young people, who have studied together through long years, who have experienced the same teacher; the class in its complete unsorted, unchosen variety. And one can have this experience in the Waldorf schools: that the more varied the pupils of a class are, the more all possible conditions of humanity are represented in it, with all kinds of backgrounds and goals and talents and interests, so much the better does the class function as a social form.

What until now the class teacher has always done, now the class does as a single unit of people. Each member of the class, with his potentialities, his weaknesses, is well-known to the others; occasionally he is treated roughly but generally he is suffered, he is carried, with amazing patience. The scale-weight that fits him and his capacity is known to them all as a matter of course. If an untalented student gives a good recitation, their criticism is different from their criticism of the work of a so-called "good" student. Where formerly the teacher learnt for the pupils, now they learn for one another. The variety of subjects makes it possible for almost every student to find at least one field in which he can be slightly ahead of the others. Those who are awkward with their hands observe with amazement how a natural craftsman handles his tools. Those who are of slower intelligence listen puzzled or even with expectant attention to the way the others take hold of a theme, illuminate it from all sides, discuss it, even often explain it to the weaker ones with great skill because they know them so well, sometimes with more success than the teacher. And when in an eleventh or twelfth grade deep questions are considered that challenge an individual's purely human maturity, then a teacher may happily experience how the weaker students, until now perhaps always very quiet, have actually learnt from the others how to enter into a discussion; often then they express themselves very decidedly and reveal a human maturity and depth that otherwise has remained hidden. And if their expression stumbles in its outer form, there will always be others in the class who out of their long common experience understand them and who now become their interpreters, to clarify their thoughts for the class and for the teacher.

In this way something can arise in the young person: trust—trust in his own capacities and trust in the others who, however different they may be, nevertheless belong to him and understand him and are understood by him. Self-confidence and confidence in his human community: this enables an individual to be a member of the social organism, and while presenting an unmistakably unique individuality himself, also to see and recognize it in the others.

With the class community is coupled another field of community experience and another meeting of destiny: the faculty of teachers, consciously working together and complementing one another, each one contributing through his particular subject to the student's broad education. What it means in social contact, in work economy and in moral support for the young person to experience his teachers not as a team of experts who have doled out the work among themselves, but as a community of educators, would be worth an article of its own. Let us limit ourselves now to the one subject, the class community.

In this sense one might now inquire into the further metamorphosis of what we have described: what the class teacher does for the children, then what the class community does for the individual—how is this continued later? The young adult must bring it to fulfillment alone. And he can if confidence in himself and trust in the world have matured in him. Then he will know how to insert his individual destiny meaningfully into the common destiny.

It is told how Rudolf Steiner said in a commencement speech to the first Waldorf School graduates: "The discussions you have had with your classmates will be the most important memory for you later on in life. Always keep coming back to them." One can well ask what this meant; why Rudolf Steiner, who had so carefully selected the curriculum for the students, disregarded it entirely in this speech. Actually, the significance of the teaching material for later life is self-evident. With the "discussions", on the other hand, can only be meant that element which I have tried to point out: the capacity that is developed through long years of practice, to see the human qualities in one another and to enter into a genuine community life with one another. This is the very strength that humanity will need in order to solve the social problems of our time.

(1975)   —Irmgard Huersch

(Translated from *"Erziehungskunst, Monatsschrift zur Pädagogik Rudolf Steiners,"* Stuttgart, June 1972, with the kind permission of the editor.)

The Teaching of Writing

Teaching the first letters to children of six or seven years old is a happy experience. Even those who already know their alphabet are delighted to follow the curve of the W in the flow of the wave and the rearing form of the snake in the S. It is not hard for them to remember letters that are taught through pictures, and they enjoy expressing them in vivid colors in their books. The real difficulty comes later, when the step has to be taken from letters to words, and when the forms and pictures have to be associated with particular sounds. At this stage it is worth while for the teacher to ponder upon the development of writing through the course of the ages; for a deeper understanding of the history that lies behind these apparently arbitrary marks, called letters, guides us in building the bridge from the learning of the alphabet to the comprehension of words and sentences.

In teaching writing we should concern ourselves not so much with the shapes of the individual letters as with the powers of understanding and movement that are called forth. We need to consider what happens in the soul life of the child when it is shown a number of meaningless signs and is told that these stand for well-known words. Or again, what happens in the bodily development when pages have to be filled with niggly black marks.

Long ago mankind had not acquired the capacities for writing and reading. Whatever forces we use to-day for these attainments could be directed to other ends, and thus the powers of picture thinking and of the spoken word were much more vivid. Only those who had gone through the strictest training so that the living quality of thought and feeling should not be lost in the abstract signs, were allowed to write. The teachers of old would have been horrified if the art of writing had been used as it is to-day for utterly trivial ends. Only that which was most lofty and sacred was worthy of being expressed, and a scribe could even be put to death if a mistake were made in transcribing the holy texts. Children when they learn to write today should also be given the impression that wonderful meanings are hidden in letters and words and that these should be written with beauty and devotion.

Speech and thought precede the written word and different qualities of thought or speech find different degrees of expression in the various alphabets. Some reveal most strongly the picture quality of thought, like the Egyptian hieroglyphics. Others are more concerned with its force and movement. For instance, in the cuneiform writing of the Chaldean epoch there is no picture quality. The wedge-shaped letters remind us of little arrows that shoot straight to the mark. The Chaldeans felt the will-element of speech that pierced the hearer with the power to hurt or heal. In the Greek alphabet we find that the growing, forming power of sound is represented. There is something sculptural in the Greek letters, and we can often feel their connections with the movements of eurythmy.

There is one ancient script that seems to have no connection with picture or sound, and this is the Ogham alphabet of the Celts. It was divorced from symbol and form, not because it was purely abstract and empty of content, but because the wisdom expressed was so sacred that none who were uninitiated must guess its meaning. The series of cuts or notches could give no hint of the mysteries they had to impart. The study of the Ogham letters is very illuminating for the teacher who would like to penetrate the processes that

97

lie behind the forming of an alphabet. The first five letters of this script are formed by a series of scratches, one, two, three, four or five, below and at right angles to a line; the next five by a similar series above a line; the next set are drawn across a line at an acute angle, and so on. No ancient alphabet appears so lifeless; yet all the letters had names, and the one who knew these knew something of their significance. Graves, Robert

Robert Graves in his book *The White Goddess* has tried to penetrate the mysteries of the Ogham letters. They all had the names of trees, and he concludes that they express what he calls a "seasonal tree magic." The first letter is named "birch," the second "'rowan," the third "ash," and so on. There are thirteen important consonants, and he relates these to the thirteen lunar months in the solar year, while the five vowels are more connected with trees related to the planets. The Druids preferred to express their alphabet by a kind of deaf and dumb language upon the fingers and only trans-ferred movements to notches on stone or wood when they had to communicate with those who were not present. Each finger was felt to have its special quality. The thumb was the most able to sense love, the first finger knowledge, the middle finger was able to foretell the weather, the fourth finger diagnosed illness, and the fifth finger was able to divine death or make a corpse to speak. We need not accept all Robert Graves' conclusions as valid, but he has under-stood that the living qualities of the trees and the seasons of the year in which they attain their strongest forces are related to the qualities of the sounds to which they give their names. We also know through eurythmy that each consonant has its special quality in connection with the passage of the sun through the twelve groups of stars. And through the nature of their sounds, consonants can work in an enlivening or a soothing way upon the soul life of the child. We learn through eurythmy also that each sound has its right and necessary form.

Picture, movement and sound—all these lie behind the letters which have now became conventional signs, and children should feel the presence of these powers when they learn to write.

Most teachers find that children differ very much in their abilities to grasp what they learn. Some more readily relate themselves to the picture element, while others are more aware of the sound. A few can form their letters very beautifully without waking to any consciousness of either picture or sound. In my own first grade I had several outstanding examples.

One little boy had a marvellous sense of color and drew the most beautifully formed letters; but if I asked him for a word beginning with the sound "t," he would as likely as not reply "goat" or "pig." For a long time he could not relate words beginning with the same sound. On the other hand, there was a little girl who loved the story and the pictures of the snake and the fish; but when she came to draw them, her snake was a series of nervous jerks and her fish was more like a sausage exploding in a pan. She had no ability to control the form of what she really understood quite well. She was, however, very musical, and had no difficulty in providing a string of words beginning with any sound she was given. A third child who came from a farm could copy his letters with lovely curves and tender colors, but he lived in a dream and never remembered what any of them meant.

We should bear all these types in mind, and, in the teaching of the letters, pictures, movement and sound must all play their part so that the different children become harmonized.

As far as the pictures are concerned, every teacher should make his own, but it is better, I think, to give those which imply movement than those that are static. The snake, the fish and the wave are all good from this point of view. For "H" the picture of a horse is more alive than that of a house, although it is very tempting to draw a pretty little cottage with two high chimneys. For "G" a goose looking back over its tail is more comical and appealing than an open gate leading into a garden.

While the children are busy developing their letters, a good deal of attention should be paid to form for its own sake. In many round games and exercises they can run straight and curved lines, and it is a good practice to let them draw or write these on a large scale, perhaps with a wet mop on the floor or a rake in the sand pit. Nearly every main lesson I used to allow some of the children in my own first grade to come in turn to draw on the blackboard. They could choose their own colors to make strong straight lines or bold curves, and soon they gained confidence and could draw with strength and certainty.

As children learn to know their letters, copying of writing should go hand in hand with words or verses which they already know by heart. Then gradually the writing takes on meaning for them. Nursery rhymes are very helpful in the first writing lessons, for children suddenly recognize with the great joy of discovery the familiar words emerging from a whole series of jumbled letters. It is inadvisable to make special sentences of very simple words so that writing may be easy for them, for this is really boring and gives them the feeling that writing has not anything very important to say. They should keep best books, and their work in these should be a very serious and solemn affair. At the same time, as soon as children begin to recognize words I think it is helpful to give them dictations of tiny phrases which they know by heart, where the letters follow the sounds fairly closely. Thus they have continual practice in listening. Children readily accept the inconsistency in spelling. The teacher can explain that every word is like a family; and just as most families have babies or old grannies who do not do any work, so most words have letters that do not make any sound. Also just as their fathers sometimes like a change from the office and choose to dig in the garden, some letters like to change their work. "C" will sometimes do the work of the king "K," but sometimes it prefers to make the sound of the snake. English spelling is certainly a handicap to quick progress in writing and reading; but perhaps it is a saving grace for the English who so love to take life easily and judge from the standpoint of common sense, that in their spelling they cannot for a single moment feel secure. Perhaps they also owe to their spelling and their involved tables of measure and weight that they are very rarely pedantic.

The chief aid to the grasp of the sound in letters should be eurythmy. It is best if a class teacher can work closely with a Eurythmist so that as the children learn to write they can also experience how movement and form are created in accordance with sound, and how poetry, which paints word pictures for the eye of the soul, can also be expressed in movement which calls to the spirit to dance.

It is a strenuous task for the teacher to help his class to unfold all the powers which lie behind the forming of the letters; but it is wonderfully worthwhile. Perhaps the greatest reward comes when a child whose faculties seemed to lie dormant suddenly begins to awake. The writing which was so crippled and ugly grows in beauty and strength; and the eyes which looked puzzled and fearful shine with a new light. May all of us who teach writing and reading take it as seriously as those masters of olden times.

(1960)   Eileen Hutchins

The article is reprinted with the kind permission of Cecil Harwood, editor of "Child and Man."

Feeling in the Growing Child

We have come to regard feelings as subjective and there-fore untrustworthy. We fight shy of them in public and are not a little ashamed of them in private. There have been parents who have asked uneasily whether our education does not encourage too much feeling for a world as hard and competitive as our own. The fact is that most people have more feeling than they know what to do with; they get distressed about little things and worry about nothings. Feeling is too often confused with emotionalism. A man of strong, deep feeling is a character; an emotional man is a type of horror. It is probably true that there is too much emotion-alism in our day and too little real feeling. Yet feeling is an essential part of human nature: a man who lacks feeling is hardly human.

Compared with thought, feeling is certainly subjective. A given thought is the same whoever thinks it, just as a given object is the same whoever beholds it. This does not apply to feeling. Even if we communicate our feelings to others, each must still feel in his own way: we can know exactly what another person thinks, we can see exactly what another person does, we can only sense approximately how the same person feels. Whether we like it or not we stand in a feeling relationship with everything around us; even indifference is a state of feeling. We feel situations, events, people, ideas, all day long, and these feelings at least color if they do not actually form our judgments. When someone concludes an argument by saying "That is how I think about it," as likely as not he means "That is how I feel about it." Because feelings are so deeply rooted in the personal, we want to be wary of them; on the other hand, to eliminate feeling from our con-duct of life leads to disaster.

If we are not to override our feelings or be over-ridden by them, we need to know them, understand them, and above all educate them. Only by educating the feeling can we hope to rise above the personal. To feel deeply may indeed mean to suffer more, but it also means to know more, to understand more, to joy more and triumph more greatly—to be more of a human being.

The greatest educator of feeling is undoubtedly art. Since art is inevitably bound up with feeling, it too is largely discredited today as being subjective. Art may *please* us, so it is argued, but it has no value in the struggle for existence. Therefore it is little more than a plaything. To spend time on art, except as a recreation, is so much waste of time. This word "recreation" is an example of how the mighty are fallen: what can be more wonderful than to re-create the human being—but that is no longer what the word means.

I have watched men and women, however, being re-created by means of art and the allied crafts. I had the good fortune to visit a place called Letchworth Village in New York where there are over four thousand "retarded" patients of all ages. Men and women of fifty, sixty and seventy years old were still called 'boys and girls.' I have seen these 'boys and girls,' mental age described as two to three years old, doing astonishing things, making lace, tapestry, rugs, a great variety of articles that would do credit to any shop window. Under the guidance of a trained and sympathetic teacher, their limbs could do what clever heads could not. By means of their work, these unhappy outcasts of modern times were reintegrated into society, were made part of the general community of man.

Here was a case not of art as pastime, not of art for art's sake, but of art for man's sake. If so much could be done through arts and crafts for the handicapped, what might not be done, by the same means, to re-create a mentally sick age where abstract minds are running ahead of human hearts: is not this whole age nervously over-wrought and crippled thereby?

Art calls for skill, form and style. Its practice educates right feeling and right judgment. True art has its source in what is invisible in us—in what makes us by our very nature more than a thing or a conditioned animal. To educate through art is to awaken human beings to their nobler attributes, to quicken their faculties for a higher perception of the world they live in.

Art makes use of matter to express that which is more than material. Poetry makes use of words to utter what is beyond the articulate. Music calls out in us another kind of hearing, the plastic arts another kind of seeing. Education should be the greatest art of all, calling out a better form of humanity. The teacher cooperates with the unexpressed genius of the child in his care, so that this hidden genius may one day speak his own language, reveal his own powers for life. In a Rudolf Steiner school all practice of the specific arts serves this all-inclusive art of education itself.

From the first grade on, in our schools, the main lesson becomes the outstanding example of an artistic method of teaching. There is nothing set. What comes about each day and in the course of weeks and years is a free creative act, according to the gifts and endeavors of the teacher in relation to the needs and capacities of his children. The ultimate goal of the whole education is that human beings shall be so helped and guided in childhood that they may, in the course of their own lives, as adults arrive at the truest possible picture of man. There is a time for listening and learning, a time for moving, clapping, reciting, practicing, conversing, a time for self-expressive individual doing, not according to the clock but as human need directs. What has been thought needs to be felt, what has been felt needs to be willed and expressed for the co-ordination of the whole human being. With the young child, the *picture* given contains the idea, for a picture can always be *felt*; young children experience the world in pictures—they *feel* the world around them long before they think about it.

Just as art selects its material with the greatest care for each particular task, so must education. The child is ever the guide. The example often quoted because it is particularly striking is that of the ninth year. Round about the ninth year when the speech center is formed, there is a gentle accentuation of the feeling of *self*: for the first time the child becomes inwardly aware that it is alone in the world. This expresses itself variously in different children: in some it leads to assertiveness, in others to a measure of fearfulness. Something must go out from the understanding adult to meet the child. The curriculum answers the situation in its own way. For example, Rudolf Steiner recommended, for the main lesson, stories from the Old Testament. These show by example the force of growing personality, the sense of purpose, of struggle and fulfillment, types of behavior and conduct, what is faithful or unfaithful, steadfast or inconsequent, courageous or cowardly—in all cases how we are intended to be the representative of something higher than ourselves. A companion period on farming shows how we live in relation to sun and moon and the seasons: to the earth beneath us, to the plants that grow and the creatures of the field; the farmer and his wife and the whole community of the farm form a picture of the wise human coordinating powers carrying purpose to expression in outer life. During this year, there is given the first important period on grammar, "the backbone of language," so that with the forming of the speech center there may also be the beginning of a more conscious use of words.

Into this general artistic method of education, which adapts itself year by year and which enters into the treatment of every subject, there comes the art work itself. Art includes recitation and drama, painting, modeling, carving, eurythmy and gymnastics, handicrafts of many kinds and other such activities. In all this work it is *the type of exercise* that is all important and the time when it is introduced. If art is over-directed it becomes mere technique. If, on the other hand, there is unlimited freedom it becomes a matter of mere self-indulgence. Both ways the true impulse of art is defeated. Art is an extended language and needs its own form of grammar, syntax and the like. The training through art in school is not for the purpose of producing artists as specialists but in order to educate young human beings for the art of living. The greatest and most liberating art is based on sober and disciplined exercise and this is equally true of great living.

The following example taken from work with six-year-olds will illustrate what is meant by exercise. The children were told a story about a star. Some days later, on their painting morning, they were to *paint* a star. What is more fitting than bright radiant yellow for a star? So the children dipped their large square brushes into the liquid paint and formed a bright yellow center on their slightly moistened paper. And now, with the same big brushes, the children beginning at the center painted the rays outwards, the yellow growing fainter as it moved further away from its source. Now, in the middle of the paper, there was this great shining star of spreading rays. But there must be something to *hold* the star there on the white paper even as the night holds the stars in the deep blue heavens. The brushes having been carefully washed clean were now dipped into liquid blue, and the children began to bring this blue, as if from the furthest heavens, to the edges of the paper. There around the edges the blue was darkest, and now, very carefully, the hand of these little six-year-olds guided the streams of blue towards the star—led the blue, growing fainter and fainter in between the golden rays, till blue touched yellow on the way to the heart of the golden star. How very carefully they had to guide the blue so that the yellow should remain clean without smudging and so that there should be no dry bare white patches left between. At length it was done and there was the star shining outwards in its yellow and the blue holding it firmly but gently in its place. Half-way through this exercise, as the blue was approaching the yellow but had not yet arrived, one of the six-year-olds was heard to say in wonder, "Look, the star is beginning to shine!" In the exercise there was care, precision, cleanliness, appreciation of the qualities of the colors used and most important, a *discovery* for the child to make!

This elementary example taken from the very young is true of the entire work which must include at each level appropriate elements of training, control, true use of material, suitable selection of the task and room for discovery. Such exercises then flow little by little into "free expression" so that at the end there is *order in freedom*—and this latter is precisely what the world lacks today. Nor will there be *order in freedom* till there is right judgment, a balance between the directing force of thought and the impelling force of will which can come only through sound, disciplined feeling.

One of the most decisive periods of childhood is the transition to adolescence. At this time there is a sudden lighting up in the thinking accompanied by a definite descent into bodily function. The one gives rise to a new feeling of independence and the other to sexual maturity. The result is a considerable tension of soul. There are authorities on delinquency who state that a great many recurring criminals began their unhappy career at this time. In the normal child the mind is open for ideas and ideals, whilst there can be at the same time a great feeling of loneliness and depression and a longing for understanding companionship. If the education is intellectual and abstract, leaving the life of feeling to its own resources, there can be much chaos of soul: feeling and will are flung back on themselves and give rise to introspection as well as to erotic impulses. The sex creed of today is the outcome of abstract thinking and unbalanced feeling. The true mood of adolescence is to reach out to the whole of life with understanding and love. The primary impulse is one of love for all creation. If, however, the world is presented as a material process only, this impulse of the soul is largely defeated and is flung back on to itself. As one practical measure the art teaching brings to the children at this time the experience of working with the dramatic medium of black and white, the contrast of light and darkness. The conflict that arises in the soul through the longing for the ideal and the sense of being body-bound finds relief in self-expression and a right self-knowledge. Art becomes the mediator and protector, the friend and healer in these diffi-cult years.

Feeling will always be subjective, but the subject may grow so that through his feelings he comes into a deeper and more direct relationship with the world of his origin and the goal of his future. When feeling bears the balance of artistic perception, it frees a person from himself, for then he may relate idea to impulse, thought to will, driven by nothing but the voice of his own heart. Such a one will also seek the hearts of all others. This will be the true strength which works through gentleness.

We live in an age when there is on the one hand too much direction, making for unfreedom, and on the other hand, too much abandonment to senseless striving and living, licen-tiousness masquerading as freedom. It is the middle factor, the balancing factor, that threatens to be eliminated, the life of soul mediating between thoughts and action, between spirit and body. The time has come for the 'pale cast of thought' to be permeated with the warm life-blood of the human heart so that there may arise a new perceiving, a new understanding and a new caring for others and the world. Science itself is coming to this point of view and is awaiting a qualitative change in human thinking. The mathematical thought of the past has produced the machine, largely at the expense of the human heart. The machine is only at the beginning of its possibilities, which are great in themselves, but we need new hearts if they are not to be overwhelmed and crushed by the force of their own inventions—and these new hearts can only be born by way of educating qualities of soul, of feeling and of will which can deepen thinking and lead human minds to behold horizons of the spirit.

(1971)   Francis Edmunds

Color in Childhood

From the moment of birth onward the child lives in a world where colors play a decisive part as strong sense impressions. A healthy child is naturally delighted when for the first time paints, paper and painting brush are put in front of him ready for his use. He has encountered colors in picking yellow buttercups, red poppies and purple violets. He has enjoyed the fresh green of the newly mown grass in spring, when the white cover of snow has long melted away and the blue sky with some fine, white feathery clouds is mirrored in the quickly flowing river.

In fairy tales the child is told of the Queen's wish to have a little daughter "as white as snow, as red as blood and as black as the ebony window-frame" or of the "golden bird with the three golden feathers." Colors help to form the imaginative pictures which so powerfully take hold of the child's soul and they reveal to him spontaneously quality and taste—the solemnity of the dark blue or the nobility of the deep red of the King's cloak, or the swift and mischievous vermilion of the frisky pony galloping fast over the hills!

About the age of six the child enters school. The curriculum given for the use of the Waldorf schools suggests for the first school year: "The child should be introduced to the world of plastic-sculptural forces by means of painting and drawing. The sense of color should be developed by experiencing pure color in its consonance and dissonance. The child can see form as being created by color."

What actually happens in the schoolroom in the time set aside for painting? The preparation is simple, but it is one of the precious moments when we instil into the growing human being the first love and reverence for his tools and materials. The sheet of painting-paper is white and clean. After dampening the surface of the painting board, a wet sponge helps to stretch the paper so that it lies completely flat on the board. Then we dissolve the paints in small pots, one for each color, and every child has his own yellow, red and blue. The broad paintbrush lies ready for use next to a jar filled with clean water.

Joyful expectancy has reached its peak in the classroom. The brush is dipped with delight into the yellow liquid and touches the white paper. Yellow starts to spread out radiantly and speaks to the child. It can be a gay tale of light. But soon something else appears: blue is moving from one corner of the paper downwards, enveloping the clean, gay yellow in a complete circle. The yellow is soon imprisoned and no ray of light can shine through the blue wall. Only the triumphant red breaks through the blue circle and starts to play with the yellow, making it strong and fiery. Every stroke of the brush performs a colorful miracle, changing colors and forms in an endless variety. The child's soul is the center of this creative activity. No wonder that he is quiet and immersed in his work. Each child is engaged in his own special conversation with the colors.

This is what the young child longs for in his first school years: to enter upon an education which is alive and imbued with an element of art.

Up to the fourth grade children should be stimulated to a genuine color-experience which will enable them later to start to paint out of their own creative phantasy. Color now becomes the means of expression for all that they learn in their lessons. With their experiences of the quality of colors, they can now paint maps; artistic work and even geography can become united. They will use different color shades when painting a map of Scandinavia than for a map of Egypt.

The healing power of colors and painting is more and more recognized. But only when the teacher has followed the development of a sequence of paintings does he become aware of the manifold difficulties on the way to achievement: to learn to guide the brush, to control the pressure, to avoid scratching the paper with the metal part of the brush, to control the over-abundance of liquid color—these belong to the initial difficulties.

In the way described, the pupil is gradually introduced to the *discipline* of painting—and I use the word "discipline" with great emphasis. In our time much stress is laid on the young child's "freedom" to choose his own materials for his first artistic ventures, out of a bewildering manifoldness The child's path to "free expression" is paved forcefully at an early age by modern teaching methods. This is done especially at the time when the school child is trying to find in his teacher one who "knows"—who knows what is beautiful, what is ugly.

Whether conscious of it or not, the child longs to be guided into color experiences by his teacher—to be told, for example, that a blue patch next to a yellow one is more beautiful than green put next to yellow. By providing the child with the right tools for his artistic work, the teacher's guidance grows into the discipline of painting and drawing. After puberty, true "free expression" can develop, and individual judgment and taste unfold. It is the well-tried way from being a pupil, to becoming an apprentice, in order to achieve mastery in artistic work.

Who would deny the urgent need for fostering these truly creative possibilities today? The first seeds can be planted by the teacher in the first painting lesson he gives to his class. And thus we can divine the responsibility of teachers of today. What we first and foremost want to achieve is to open the mind of the child for the true quality of the colors, to give him the exciting experiences of red and blue and yellow and green, and to let him partake as fully as possible in the healing truth: "Color is a manifestation of life revealed by the spirit."

(1970)   Trude Amann

Reprinted with the kind permission of THE CRESSET, *Journal of the Camphill Movement, Christmas, 1969.*

How Eurythmy Works in the Curriculum
An Answer to a Question Asked by an Elementary School Parent

The 'blueprint' of the idea behind a Rudolf Steiner school lies in the planning for each subject to be taught in relation to the right age of the child. This 'Waldorf School Curriculum' is a living organism, guiding the teachers in a broad and creative way, from kindergarten through the twelfth grade, and emphasizing the importance all along of applied imagination. Eurythmy comes in as a great help at every age level. In eurythmy we learn to control movement by means of rhythm and form. Eurythmy is controlled movement.

Practically every eurythmy lesson in all the grades begins with the forming of a circle—not just standing in a circle but actively forming it together, the teacher and all the pupils present. It is an image of wholeness in balance; it combines form, movement and rhythm in one gesture. As soon as the circle begins to move, swinging to the right, to the left, in toward the center—becoming very small, or out toward the periphery—becoming larger and larger, there is rhythm. The circle, as a balance between all these directions, contains every possible rhythm. Rudolf Steiner speaks about rhythm as 'the healer'; we try to have rhythm in everything we do in school, particularly in the elementary school years.

The swinging rhythms we do on the circle can lead us directly into the musical part of eurythmy, tone eurythmy, and at the same time can give us structure and form. The better we learn to mould the form, the more we are free to swing and sing rhythmically in the movement. If we can build a really firm eurythmy circle together, we can also let the 'builders' run loose in a free eurythmy swing and quite easily bring them back to order. In the lower grades it is better that each child has his own definite place on the circle line, whereas it is good for the older children to stand in different places and thus have to create a new circle every time. They will then benefit from the selfless activity employed in forming a harmonious circle together with everyone else in the class. It may take time but it will give strength to the continuation of the lesson.

These rhythmic movements on the circle are done in a very simple way in first and second grade. Gradually the children become able to develop more complicated rhythmic form-patterns in the following years.

In the first grade we work with the colorful pictures of the fairy tales, whose rich material is needed at this age to nourish the imagination. The king and queen are given their dignified steps and eurythmy gestures. The changing over from the rushing of the wicked witch to the graceful movement of the princess is in itself a powerful rhythm. This approach to rhythm, the lively change from one quality to another, rather than by clapping or stepping out syllables with the feet, is altogether fitting for this age, when the children still dwell in dreamy pictures.

To make them experience the change from contraction to expansion, the teacher might let the children dive into and live for a long while in the element of contraction and then let them realize the relief of expansion, a change from the picture of something dark, heavy, narrow, tight, or sad into the opposite, bright, light, wide: letting them perhaps as dwarfs crouch down and with tiny, tense steps hammer their way through a narrow passage ... and then come to a bright opening where, becoming swallows, they can soar out over the sunny meadow in free-flowing flight.

These fairy tale images will then also suggest an immediate movement of the various consonants and vowels, without naming them as letters. Even in the second grade, where we continue with fairy tales, adding the fables and legends, we avoid giving a movement the name of a letter, waiting rather until the child is ready to discover it himself. In that way he will be able to enjoy the movement with an aura of imagination around it, instead of dropping it down to the level of intellect. The animal stories lend themselves particularly well to the experience of the movement of a consonant.

We can characterize each wonderful animal in a concrete manner right down into our feet. There is a whole world of intangibles in the difference between the child who performs the mighty D. . D. . of the elephant foot being placed on the ground, and the child depicting the dainty d. .d. .d. .d. . of the hopping robin, the sneaky n. .n. .n. . of the fox or the heavy, warm B. .B. . of the good brown bear.

As we continue the rhythmic work in second and third grades, we can also make use of nursery rhymes which bring all kinds of rhythms both for stepping and clapping, as well as a rich variety of words and images. It is now time to become more secure with regard to left and right, and we can use the ringing, swinging bells of so many nursery rhymes to develop quite skillful changes from left to right,—even with two children together, swinging in various directions and rhythms.

In the third grade these exercises are brought further, expanding the movement to a larger reach and better control. The third grader's imagination reaches right up to heaven with the Bible stories, as he learns at the same time to build his house here on earth. He also experiences these two 'reaches' in eurythmy, where his movement can swing out freer at this age than later on when the intellect may hold him back. It is expanding and freeing for the children to move and breathe eurythmically with the glorious largeness of the psalms, while at the same time they are learning precision and firmness in rhythmic stepping with their legs and feet.

These two opposite reaches can come closer and closer in the development of the child until he wakes up to a stronger self-awareness (and often becomes a nuisance to himself and others!). The far reaches change as the fourth-graders come a step further down to earth and now learn about the difference between man and animal—or in the language of eurythmy form: they come into the square. The squareness is a rather rigid condition in which the fourth-grader can be guided to 'controlled freedom' in becoming aware of the four directions of space—in geography they are learning about their home town. In eurythmy, moving forward is an entirely different experience from moving backwards or sideways; in moving to the right, the child will feel strength and up-sweep; in moving to the left, he can express inwardness and stillness. Working up to a certain security within the square-ness and the four directions, the fourth-grader slowly develops into a fifth-grader and will then be ready to free himself from the square and from the circle.

There will be less and less the need to face the center of the circle or the need to be sustained by the class unit represented in the circle. He may now stand in a place where the four directions meet, within himself, freed from the class unit, facing forward. This is rather an important moment in the child's development, when he begins to look differently at the world around him. He is still 'behind the fence', as it were, but beginning to peep over it into the world.

In this transition toward self-awareness the child is getting ready for the rod exercises, for which up to now he has been carefully prepared, without getting into any particular 'body correction.' The fifth-grader excels in rod exercises as he grows more firmly into his body. He now reaches out to the palm of his hand, so to speak, and from now on we can require more active forming with the hand. In the work on dramatic poetry or music and in the experience of major and minor music, we have a wonderful opportunity to let the children enjoy the two contrasting forces of expansion and contraction that are alive in them. The fifth grade corresponds to the age of the balanced Greek, and we swing easily in the harmonious lemniscate (one of the eurythmy forms suggested by Rudolf Steiner), realizing that the supple grace will soon disappear when the children reach the sixth grade.

The sixth-grader has come even deeper down into his body and is open to law and order (in spite of his violent opposition toward it!). The curriculum calls for Roman history and geometry. In eurythmy we deal with geometric forms in all variations. The work we have done up to now with geometric forms has been more out of a sense of flow;

now in the sixth grade we concern ourselves with the shaping and the precision of the form. The underlying laws, too, of a poem or piece of music are being studied and brought out in eurythmic movement. This can lead us to the understanding of the ballad form, which is scheduled for the seventh grade and which gives the boys and girls full opportunity to express the soul-filled moods of poetry. The children at this age experience intimately the realm of the inner soul-life, at the same time that they are brought into contact with the laws of the star world in the study of astronomy. Both realms, inner and outer, can be expressed in eurythmy, the one through definite gestures characterizing a variety of soul moods and soul conditions, such as expectation, inwardness, hope, longing, love, etc., the other through moving in geometric forms or according to the grammatical structure of language.

The eighth grade is given the opportunity to develop further in this direction and to work strongly at the sculptural quality of language from many different aspects. This can awaken the eighth grader to a balance between the outside world around him and the inner turmoil in which the girls and boys so often find themselves at this age. The work with these opposites helps to lead them to the inner security so needed when they reach high school age.

In the high school classes, the young people follow the poets and poetry of the various historical epochs. Now they can approach eurythmy with more artistic detail: expressive positions and movements of feet and hands, the heightened use of the laws of color, a deeper study of music; everything is raised to a more conscious level. As the curriculum moves forward in a spiral fashion, it touches again on the elements already studied in the lower grades.

Now it becomes more and more evident that eurythmy is not just a study for itself, as an intriguing school subject, but it is the means by which every child can be helped in his whole development. Thus throughout all the school years the eurythmy curriculum follows closely the main lesson

curriculum, for this is adjusted to the development of consciousness at the various stages of the child's life.

(1974)   Kari van Oordt

Children's Play

Whoever observes children today will declare that their
capacity for play is gradually disappearing. They are not able
to play as children used to play. Play has always been the
archetypal characteristic of childhood and it is in danger of
vanishing. Either it manifests as wild, unrestrained rushing
about, or a child droops and settles into a state of impassive
dullness.

This phenomenon should be taken very seriously. For it is
an alarm signal, pointing to a profound and devastating
change in the constitution of children. Children who cannot
play are ill in a certain sense. They may not show symptoms
immediately that are clinically clear, but they are in a condition that without question must lead later to soul weaknesses
and bodily illnesses.

You hear so often today: our children no longer like the old
ways of playing; they want something more realistic. Even
if this is true, one should work against it. The old kinds of
play, so full of fantasy, are not out-of-date, they are not
superfluous, they are really right and good. They are in the
same class as fairy tales. Fairy tales are important for a child's
soul because they have a timeless quality. And it is this
quality of timelessness that one finds in genuine play.

How, then, should our children play? The answer must
surely be: so that their whole being is involved. But since
different faculties keep unfolding as the children grow, the
character of their play has also to change continually; there
must always be some new element appearing to correspond
to the children's development.

An important element of play is the sandbox. There the child's formative forces have a chance to be active, the forces that are working on his entire body during his first seven years. During those years every human being is actually a sculptor and has therefore a natural impulse to busy himself as such. His hands want to move, they want to be shaping things, and it is a blessing at this time if the very forces that are working sculpturally on his entire bodily form can also be used by him in his own activity. Sand play allows him to be creative in a way that rarely can be reached again. But a seed is planted there that can ripen later into artistic originality. Teachers should grasp every opportunity to make sand play available to the children, primarily during their first four years but also later.

Up to a child's eighth year it is still comparatively easy to get him to play. However, one condition must be fulfilled: an environment must be provided that lures him to play in it. During these early years he absorbs qualities of the spatial world with tremendous intensity. He experiences "things" not as dead objects but as living bodies. When he is older he will want to grasp the world with his intellect; now he wants to grasp it not only with his hands but with his whole body. He climbs, slides, crawls, rolls, holds something fast, springs away from it. Behind all the variety of his activity is his inner need to touch the world, to feel it, to have direct contact with it, to get as close to it as possible. Forces of purest sympathy are manifesting themselves in this behavior. One could say, play is nothing less than love for the world.

The child loves the thing he is crawling through, the thing he is climbing on, and his love increases with each new encounter he has with it. The energy of his fresh young soul streams out into the world, and he receives what he gives. A mound of earth perhaps ten feet high is "his mountain." That is no pile of dirt, it is something thoroughly alive. He knows its true nature and treats it as a friend.

Children need such living relationships, for it is through them that soul faculties unfold. Obviously this can happen all the more easily, the more character the environment has in which they live. Tenements, backyards, asphalt, bare lots, even empty lawns, offer children precious little inducement to play.

Trees, bushes, a ditch, a "mountain," unexpected places to climb on or crawl through, logs or fat rocks that one can run between, climb over, jump from, by lucky chance an old boat—all offer a thousand play possibilities. This is only to suggest the direction one's thoughts should take. Under no circumstances should sophisticated technical things or machines be brought in, because a child's hidden forces can have no connection with them. One should provide for him nothing more and nothing less than "a world in miniature," of a natural, primitive, archetypal character.

The usual playground equipment—swings, slides, etc., should whenever possible not be made only of steel. Children need a certain quality of warmth that steel does not possess. Wood does possess it. And so, for instance, it makes a decided difference whether a swing is built from sturdy pieces of oak or is just a prefabricated, tubular steel affair such as one sees everywhere today. In the former event the swing has "a look," it has "character"; in the latter, it has none. For the child-soul this is not unimportant.

Singing games and free play belong together as do sleeping and waking. In free play the children follow their own impulses; in singing games they follow one another in some arranged order. All our traditional singing games have an echo of ritual in them. They may consist of the simplest words, or verses without any apparent sense. With their bare melodies they seem to be nothing more than a kind of singsong. And yet they work magic in a child's soul. Truly we are offering a genuine healing element when we give a child some regular opportunity to dip down into this activity. And it is precisely today's child that needs this to a special degree: because he is already far too awake. Overstimulation, which is steadily increasing, makes our children nervous and excitable. A singing game with its constant quiet repetitions means more for them than we could guess. Rhythmic repetition strengthens the will; continually changing impressions weaken it.

(1978)   Rudolf Kischnick

From "Merkblätter zur Gesundheitspflege" *(Number 10) published by the Verein für ein erweitertes Heilwesen, Bad Liebenzell, Germany, with their kind permission. Translated by Gladys Hahn.*

Modelling as the Expression of the Child's Inner Being

After the change of teeth, formative forces loosen themselves from the body of the child, in which they have worked until now, and press on to new activities. Knowledge of the transformation of these forces, as observed and described by Dr. Rudolf Steiner, is fundamental for pedagogical work. These liberated forces not only enable the child to learn writing, painting and drawing, but they also help him to build concepts and to keep impressions in his memory.

As these sculpturing forces long for an outlet in work, it is good to let the children, in their first school years, do some modelling from time to time. The desire to knead something into shape streams out of their very finger-tips. For this reason modelling presents a particularly good opportunity to study how these formative forces work in the child.

When we started modelling in the first grade, our subject was the figure of a little child. To begin with each child took a ball of beeswax, of a color chosen by himself, and held it in his hand. Just then I was called away from the class and was forced to leave the children alone.

I was greatly surprised when I returned. One boy had formed a figure in red wax with two giant arms spread out in the air and two long legs—and—nothing else! I asked him: "Have you finished? Isn't there something lacking in your man? Just look at yourself and see!" But the boy did not notice that his figure had no head.

He was a strange child. I will describe him briefly. From the first day he was a disturbing element in the class. Fundamentally he had a good heart, but before he himself was aware of it he would kick someone. His actions lacked consciousness, as if his will acted of itself without being directed by thought or reason. He was really headless, like his figure, which actually presented a picture of the forces that especially dominated him. In temperament he was choleric. His ungovernable will caused much disturbance in his environment. And yet, in the gestures of the figure he made was contained such splendid activity. At my suggestion this boy was allowed to beat the rugs at home.

In the work of another boy the opposite pole was shown. The head of his figure was over-large and the arms and legs were mere stumps. This child lived in an inner world of his own; he was a dreamer. He moved like a snail, but his soul was filled with the most beautiful pictures. As he had narrow, flat feet, he often fell; but if you asked him what he would like to be he would beam and say, "An astronomer".

The following incident in this boy's school life was very characteristic. On one occasion, when his class was to act out the fairy tale of the shepherd boy, we were looking for someone who would be good in the part of the king. After class, this boy said to me in a low voice, "You must make me the king for, first, I know how a king speaks, and, secondly, how he walks." And though he had formerly had certain difficulties in speaking, he played the part of the king successfully through the living quality of his imagination. When the golden crown was given to him, after the play, he experienced his greatest thrill.

Thus this child lived strongly in his imagination, in the forces of his head. He had, in fact, a huge head; so, in this case too, the figure he made was a true reflection of the

121

distribution of forces in the child. The two examples are polarities.

One remembers the description Rudolf Steiner gave of the arrangement of the human organization. He described the head organization with the nerve-sense system as the seat of thinking; the breast organization with the rhythmic functions as the physical basis for feeling; and the limb and metabolic system as the bearer of the will. He showed graphically how the preponderance of one or the other pole might bring about one-sided types.

Thus the small creations of two children bore witness to a fundamental law and in them the two poles of the threefold human organization were convincingly manifested.

A third example lies between the two which we have already considered. It again was the work of a very vigorous boy. But the child had a phlegmatic streak in his choleric temperament. His outbursts were not quite so chaotic as those of the first boy, and though he also struck out around him, he was on the whole more considerate. One could say: "To the extent that the small cone-shaped head rose above the huge form of his wax figure, to that extent was he more considerate."

A plump, easy-going little girl of phlegmatic temperament gave me her work with a beaming look. She had produced the amusing form of a little child with a small stomach like a ball, emphasized by a row of carefully placed buttons. The similarity between the little girl and the plastic figure is, in this case, so striking that no further comment is needed.

A fifth figure, bent-over and contracted into itself, was the work of a melancholic child. Here, too, a definite connection seemed to exist between the temperament of the child and his work.

The temperament is closely bound up with the distribution of forces within and, as these latter function in the child, so they pour themselves into his work, making it a small reproduction of himself which can reveal much and be of great help to the teacher. In these first lessons, with seven year old children, the connection between the inner nature and outer expression can be seen clearly.

Not only are the finished figures characteristically differentiated but also the methods of working show characteristic differences. Once, when the fairy tale of the White Snake was told, the children were supposed to form the shell with the ring inside, which the three fishes bring to land. As the children were grouped according to their temperaments, one could observe their characteristic ways more easily than otherwise. One whole group, after having formed the shell, tried to give it a richly decorated edge, working diligently with the very tips of their fingers. This was the group of sanguine children, children who move their heads as quickly as birds, who discover everything at once, but who have no perseverance. Most of them had slender bodies, delicately shaped limbs and wide-awake senses. Such children live, for the most part, in their nerve and sense system. Their experiences touch only the surface, the periphery of their bodies. It was very evident in this lesson how consciously they lived in their sense of touch, how their vitality extended to their very fingertips.

Opposite to them sat some children who dug and bored into the wax with their thumbs, even with their fists. They worked hard, with red and earnest faces. They found satisfaction in modelling deeply hollowed-out forms with thick, clumsy margins. One child, in his zeal, had even bored right through the bottom of his wax. The work of hollowing out was the chief interest of this group. For the sanguine children that was too difficult. As the wind ruffles the water, so they liked to mould only the surface.

The second group consisted of the cholerics. They live more within their bodies. They are connected less with their senses than with their blood. These are the children who, at the beginning of the lesson, enjoy warming up the cold, hard wax with their hands. They like to help with their warm fists when some other child cries: "My wax does not feel soft!"

123

From a pedagogical point of view one can accomplish a great deal in these lessons. For instance, a girl from the sanguine group said she had finished. The margin was beautifully decorated, but in the middle the wax was thick and unformed, the shell was flat. This child, then, had to accustom herself to dig down more vigorously into the wax. Or one showed a boy, who had made a deep, heavy shape, the beautiful margin of another child's form, saying: "You should decorate yours just as nicely." And so the clumsy boy had to try to make his fingers delicate and mobile.

Most of the children had formed an open shell boat. A melancholic girl gave me her work, of white wax, the shell of which was closed. Only through a narrow slit could one see the ring. She was told: "When the shell is closed, the ring cannot shine out over the water." The little girl understood this and opened her shell.

To the boy who had made a headless figure it was a great shock when, at last, he saw that his figure had no head. To the other children it was merely amusing. They just cried: "He has forgotten the head!" But to the boy himself it was a shock—and wholesome.

Help given in this way penetrates more deeply into the being of a child than many words. And it is possible, in the modelling class, to make something clear through the shaping of the forms, through the action itself. This works back upon the child, perhaps even into his physical body. Not only do children in their modelling reveal the formative forces working in them, but also it is possible through modelling to work back upon these forces in a healing and transforming way, and to build up, in the course of the lessons, a picture of the living, harmonious human being.

(1946)   Dr. Elisabeth Klein

Translated by Christiane Sorge from "Erziehungskunst", published by the Stuttgart Waldorf School, December 1931.

*If one knows that our intellect is not developed by a direct approach,
by directly working to develop the intellect; if one has observed that
someone who moves his fingers clumsily also has a 'clumsy'
intellect with not very mobile and flexible ideas and thoughts, while
he who knows how to move his fingers properly also has mobile and
flexible thoughts and ideas which can enter into the essential
nature of things, then one will not undervalue what it means to
first develop the outer skills and faculties and will realize that with
everything we do to first develop the outer activities we permit the
intellect to ripen and then to emerge as an harmonious aspect of
the whole human being.*

Rudolf Steiner
(The Renewal of Education, Lecture 5)

Handwork in the Early Grades

We all know that handwork and crafts are part of the twelve-
year curriculum of a Rudolf Steiner school, but why are they
considered so important, and what do the children learn in
the early grades beyond a few simple techniques of knitting,
crocheting and sewing?

Rudolf Steiner said that play is to the young child what
work is to the adult, the main difference being that play
comes out of the inner needs of the child, while work is
determined more from the needs of the outside world. The
kindergarten child is extremely creative and puts tremendous force and intensity into all his play. This play, this inner
force, properly guided, becomes the basis for truly creative
work and thought in the adult. "It is the task of the school
gradually to lead over from play to work" (Rudolf Steiner),
and so to develop a real connection between the child's inner
world and the outer world. One of the important bridges
between these two is the handwork lesson in the early
grades.

Making things, using materials from nature, makes one aware of all that the world has to give. For this reason it is important that the child be given natural fibers to work with. He should develop respect and appreciation for the earth out of which grows the cotton that magically becomes a potholder, wonder for the trees that give him his knitting needles, and great love for the sheep whose warm fleece becomes the wool he knits into his soft scarf. These are the seeds for understanding all that man and nature can do together and how human beings depend on one another. In this way, a true social impulse is born.

When a child makes something he can use or wear, such as a pair of socks, and makes a connection with something that would otherwise remain outside his conscious experience, he again becomes closer to the outside world and makes a step toward wholeness. It is a problem of our times that people feel cut off from their surroundings. To know how the ordinary things we use in life come into being makes one less of a stranger in one's environment.

But nothing can happen in a handwork lesson unless one works with one's hands! The will must be used, and happily for the child he can quickly see the results of his efforts. He gains confidence in himself as he sees a simple ball of yarn turn into a hat he can wear home. Why be afraid of the world when one can do so much with so little? I think it is important, therefore, that the children make things in which they can start from the beginning, and do every step themselves. No ready-made patterns, no hidden steps by the teacher. How does something get turned inside out? How did that cord get through the top of that drawstring bag? Many things that children used to see and learn at home they are completely ignorant of today. They are thrilled and excited by these magical tricks. All this stimulates their inventive powers and the ability to have creative ideas when facing the unknown. We know how much they will need these capacities in the world they will face as adults.

What is handwork in a kindergarten? This question often comes up and I think has to be deeply examined in the light of child development. The sense of order, form, color and beauty in dealing with the materials of the world is expressed by the kindergarten child in the care with which he sets the table, chooses the mat to go under the candle, places his two shoes together in a row with others, or neatly folds his sweater before putting it away. That is handwork for the child before the change of teeth. Learning a real craft draws him away too soon from his imaginative, creative world. Far better that he will sit down with two sticks or pencils and imitate the adult knitting than that he learns to do one or two things with threads.

It is different when it comes to first grade. Something more is happening. The child has reached the dawn of his intellectual thinking and in the handwork class he now really learns to knit.

Rudolf Steiner said, "Thinking is cosmic knitting": the continuous thread of thinking weaves itself into whole thoughts. How can we enhance the cooperation between the hands and the head? We must call upon the feelings. Color awakens interest, enthusiasm and joy in the child. He should be given the beautiful colors he so eagerly responds to in nature. He must develop a sensitivity toward colors, really observe them, and be aware of how they affect one another. A bright yellow thread cries out to be made into a golden chain. The child responds and the activity of the limbs works with the feelings and stimulates the processes of the head. It should become a harmonious, rhythmical activity. The child must begin to be conscious. He counts his stitches; he must know when one is missing. There is a right way to hold the needles, a right time to put the thread over the needle. Such things slowly bring the child out of his unconscious world.

In the second grade, still using the continuous thread, we crochet shapes, a kind of early geometry—a rectangular potholder, a round pocketbook, a five-cornered mat. Are the sides equidistant? The child must develop judgment and a sense of form and space. Learning of this kind can have a real balancing effect on his whole being. It awakens feelings in the child who is one-sidedly intellectual, stimulates activity in the weak-willed child, and awakens the thinking in the dreamy child.

To bring about this balanced effort of all the child's forces is a tremendous challenge to the handwork teacher. She must call upon her own powers of imagination, enthusiasm and play. Then the child will happily participate, and along with all the hidden lessons of life, he will learn the practical skills of knitting, crocheting and sewing.

"Children who learn while they are young to make practical things by hand in an artistic way, and for the benefit of others as well as themselves, will not be strangers to life or to other people when they are older. They will be able to form their lives and their relationships in a social and artistic way, so that their lives are thereby enriched."*

(1976)   Patricia Livingston

In Third Grade

The realities of time and space as the adult knows them are foreign to a six-year-old. A first grader may announce grandiosely: "I used to suck my thumb when I was little!"— meaning until last week. He can't wait for his next birthday—eleven months from now. "When are we going home?" he may ask plaintively 30 minutes after the school day has started. He is, in fact, very close still to the age that knows only two tenses: 'Now,' and 'Not now.'

His grasp of spatial distance is equally elusive. A foot-sized doll may be crammed into a six inch doll bed simply because she ought to have a nap now. Fred Gipson tells of a day in his childhood when he decided to climb the mountain in back of his house, only to find it a day's walk away.

* *Hedwig Hauck,* HANDWORK AND HANDICRAFTS: *Part I. Translated by Graham Rickett. Steiner School Fellowship, 1968.*

By the third grade the child's experience of time and distance begins to approximate our own. He *doesn't* need his sneakers *this* week any more, because the next gym class is on *Monday*. He may still guess a door to be 3 feet, or 20 feet high, but when he sees the teacher standing eloquently in the doorway he can adjust his guess to come close to the measurable dimensions of the door.

With this new-found way of seeing the outer world comes a growing awareness of an inner world, shut off from the outer. A nine-year-old has dreams and memories and can recognize them as such. He feels himself a person unlike any other, often misunderstood . . . *Shades of the prison-house begin to close upon the growing boy* . . .

The curriculum for the third grade in a Waldorf school includes stories from the Old Testament. Adam is cast out of Paradise and must earn his bread by the sweat of his brow. Moses must lead his people in the wilderness. David can subdue Goliath.

In Rudolf Steiner's suggestions for the third grade we find that he advocates the study of matters of practical life. The hints are few. Children should learn the duties of a farmer, care of the soil, the different food grains, etc. They should become acquainted with the steps in house building,—bricklaying, mortar-making.

From such hints whole units of study in 'Farming' and 'Housing' have evolved. At many Waldorf schools a three or four week block of the main lesson—the first double period every morning—is in the third grade dedicated to the subject of Housing. What follows is an attempt to outline such a block.

As a teacher looks for certain rhythmical pulsebeats of expansion and contraction, movement and contemplation, joy and sorrow to pervade each lesson, so does he look for a similar dynamics in the structure of a whole unit of study. In our block on Housing the first day or two were thus given over to, as it were, global considerations; the main part of the unit was concerned with the steps and details involved in

129

building a house such as we live in; the last two or three days were spent considering how people around the world build their houses in accordance with climate and available materials.

First, then, we talked about how the whole earth is a home—if not a house—that all men share; the rock-foundation providing a solid flooring, the vaulted sky a roof overhead. We considered, too, how each of us lives in his own body as in a house, with the sense organs in the head for windows and doors through which to communicate with the world.

When we came to the study of how a house is built we first followed the biographies of the materials, giving one day's lesson to each of the more important ones. One day the children learned about lumber, from the seedling in a great northern forest to the truck-delivered beams at the building site. Another day was spent on the life-story of a brick, from the digging of the clay to the final placing in a bond named according to its pattern. The children heard descriptions of the mining of iron ore, the smelting, the casting of girders. This was followed by a day learning about quarrying, masons' tools, dressed stone.

When 26 nine-year-olds vividly imagine what they hear, the atmosphere in the classroom becomes charged with the content of the lesson. There was a green, outdoor feeling of the woods in the room as we spoke of the forester, the look-out man in the fire tower, the lumberman. The temperature seemed to rise when the blast furnaces were our topic. The air became dry and dusty as the mason dressed the stone. Yet when I asked the children later where they would like to work if they were given a choice, the vote for the forest was by no means unanimous. Many were challenged by the heat and noise of a foundry; some felt attracted even to work in the pits of a mine.

After about a week of thus getting to know the materials, the construction of a house was followed step by step, from the choosing of a site and consultations with the architect to the finished home and the housewarming party, with various customs of blessings, offering of bread and wine, etc. We then compiled a list of people involved in the actual building. It was a good experience to see how many helpers are needed for us to live as we do.

We were not able to do any building ourselves, but we visited the construction site of the house of a classmate, saw the exposed wiring, bundles of insulating material, plumbing fixtures not yet in place; we climbed up raw staircases, and we watched masons dressing the stones of the facing of the house. Before we left we recited a house-blessing that we had learned in the classroom.

Such a unit of study provides much factual information and new terminology, which children of this age take up with zest. It also affords practice in arithmetic, scale-drawing, composition—and letter-writing. It can broaden cultural horizons. It engenders gratitude, both to the natural world and to our fellow-men for their services, and respect for materials and human skills.

It also allows confidence to grow. At the end of our studies, one third grade boy went home to tell his mother, "If I had the materials now, I could build you a house!"

(1971)   Susanne Berlin

A Teacher Talks to her Children

During the summer our class has been widely separated. Some of you have traveled thousands of miles from New York, for one was in Europe, another in California and still another in Mexico. Several children escaped the heat by going to the mountains, and at least four of you were swimming in the ocean off Long Island or the Jersey coast. But I stayed right here in New York, and because I was here you were all here with me. Oh, to be sure, I have not seen any of you for a quarter of the year with my real eyes, but here in my mind's eye you have been present many times.

And what did I see when I thought of you? Not the unimportant things, certainly nothing unpleasant which would best be forgotten, but I saw again and again in my mind's eye what I like to think of as the golden moments of our class. I remember one beautiful spring day in Central Park when all of you played leapfrog together, starting at the top of the hill and going all the way to the bottom. You were all happy and laughing, and when it was time to go back to school, everyone talked about what a wonderful time you had had. Then, there was a day when we were rehearsing for our play and several were absent and we realized we might have to give the play at the big assembly with several of our important grasshoppers and ants missing. And every one of you worked so hard making the last minute changes, and suddenly we realized there was nothing to worry about, for each child could be depended upon to do his very best, and that was all that was necessary. Another picture came to my mind, too. A child visited our class and he felt strange and ill at ease, but he was greeted with warmth and friendliness. He was shown where to go and what to do. Supplies were generously given him by his neighbors, and you all tried to make him feel at home so successfully that he begged his mother to let him come to our school, and here he is with us in our new year. I remember a little girl who hurt herself in the park and tried to pretend it was nothing at all. But I thought it was serious enough for us all to go back to school right away so that she could be properly attended to. You immediately understood the emergency and were full of sympathy for the little girl and I heard not one word of complaint that we had to miss half our recess. These are just a few of our golden moments; there are many more.

This gift to remember and relive again and again whatever impresses us is common to all human beings. It is the means by which mankind is able to pass on to future generations the golden moments of the different ages. Long before time was even recorded people told of the great events they had seen, when good had triumphed over evil, when warm-heartedness had won the prize from cleverness or when courage conquered cowardliness. These happenings were told over and over and they have come down to us in the form of fairy tales with the edge of reality blurred, but the great truths still shining. In first grade we relived these golden moments of so very long ago.

In another civilization, an old African slave told stories that so impressed his listeners that they had to repeat them to their families and to all their friends. These tales lived in the minds of many people until at last they were written down, and today when we hear Aesop's Fables, we recapture with inner vision the same pictures the Greeks formed in their minds.

Many years ago, before tales were written down, a small group of people living in a tiny corner of the world felt such deep reverence for the great men among them that they had to tell about them and their deeds to all they knew. Around their fires at night they told their sons about the nobleness of their leaders and these sons told their sons in turn. They spoke with such vigor and enthusiasm that vivid, dramatic, colorful pictures formed in the minds of all who heard. At last, when the stories were already ancient, they were written down and became the Old Testament of the Bible, for these people were the ancient Hebrews. Their golden moments have become one of the world's greatest treasures. In Third Grade we shall share this treasure.

I doubt very much if Aesop and his Greek listeners, or the ancient Hebrews were in the least bit aware that they were preparing a treasure for mankind. They were merely keeping alive in their minds' eye those events, those people, those stories which meant a great deal to them. It makes us realize how important this gift of having inner pictures is. The way we think of our friends, the stories we repeat, the moments in our lives that we think of over and over again are very significant. For each one of us in this way is helping to prepare our gift for mankind. It is up to all of us to see that our gift is a treasure worth having.

(1955)   Virginia Paulsen

Children's Song

The light of the sun is flooding
the realms of space;
the song of birds resounds
through fields of air;
the tender plants spring forth
from Mother Earth,
and human souls rise up
with grateful hearts
to all the spirits of the world.

Rudolf Steiner
From *The Portal of Initiation*

Beginning Bible Stories

Telling Bible stories to the children in their third year in the Rudolf Steiner School is an experience one would like to share with everyone who loves children. But one can only do this in part, for the reverence and awe of small children can not adequately be written down, even in the "Bible Books", which they make with such joy and care. A visitor to the class could not fully share this experience for it is revealed only in the exchange of ideas and picture thoughts between the teacher and the children. Rudolf Steiner has often told us that little children live naturally immersed in religion, and one feels this vividly when seeing and hearing their response to the unfolding of the story of Creation. Children love the Bible language and it works strongly on them as they copy such quotations as, "And God said,'Let there be light.' " From the first lessons the children, among themselves, chose to print the name of God in shining yellow, for yellow light has been associated with goodness and wisdom from their earliest color lessons. After the careful copying of verses, each day of Creation was illustrated in color with a fearless spontaneity no ordinary adult could hope to achieve.

On the first day of Bible study these children, whose creative imaginations have been stimulated and developed through fairy stories and fables with their inner meanings, sat before the teacher with trusting, glowing faces. She realized more than ever before that if she was to give them what they needed, she must call on the deepest understanding and wisdom of which she was capable. To bring the children into the right mood it was enough to point to the word "Holy" on the cover of the Bible and to tell them that it had been written long, long ago by wise old men. They were told that long before the stories had been written down they had been told by the old men to their sons and by the sons to their sons, and so on through many generations. The teacher did her best to give the feeling of travelling back through aeons of time, to the darkness with God hovering over it, "thinking in his heart" that he would create light. Then the first day of Creation was read from the Bible amid a solemn hush.

Each new day began by the children's reading aloud from their own Bible Books, which they did in such a serious way that the teacher could plainly see that "holiness" is a real state to them.

One day before the whole story of Creation was completed, a little girl stopped her careful printing and sat brooding for awhile. Finally she asked, with a dreamy look on her face, "How could the wise old men know what to write down when no one but God was there at first?" The whole class stopped work to learn the answer. A teacher must respond to such a question with complete truth in the form best suited for a child. And so it seemed quite natural and sufficient when she told them that the wise old men went apart to a lonely place where God and his angels told them what to write. An unexpected reaction to the mood of holiness occurred on another day when a little boy appeared in class with no picture for his Bible Book. He said he had lost the paper which the teacher had given him to draw it on. Acting overhastily, the teacher began to scold him for not doing it on something else, but the child broke in with the protest, "But I couldn't use just *any* paper for a Bible picture!" This shows again that a teacher must always have her most delicate feelers out to know what lies as a reality behind childish acts.

From the almost unimaginable reaches of time passed in Creation we came at last to the Garden of Eden. The story of the beautiful garden and man's leaving it is a living reality to children nearing the age of eight. For at this age they are leaving their own Paradise, where they have lived in fairytale beauty and perfection, and are descending slowly into the practical, workaday world. As one child wrote, "They were sent out of the Garden and then they had to work." The actual words do not convey all that this meant to the child, but their significance lies in the fact of her choosing just that aspect of the story. Yet if the children have had their rightful heritage of wisely chosen stories, they carry with them an imagination and a memory of Paradise

136

and the desire to find again some day what one little boy called, "The Garden of Goodness". The third chapter of Genesis is so complete a story that after reading it the moment seemed to have arrived to let the children recreate it for themselves, on paper. To their great joy they were allowed to go ahead with their own versions of the story and each one showed very clearly what parts had impressed him the most.

Though the telling of Bible stories is not to be confused with religious instruction, the mood of the children is such that the teacher can easily make a lasting impression on them at this time, laying a foundation for real moral feeling in the future. They have already dimly experienced the rightness of the good and beautiful young prince and princess overcoming wicked enchantments and fierce dragons, to live happily ever afterward. It seems natural to them that the youngest son, though not clever like his brothers, should accomplish the difficult tasks through goodness of heart and simplicity. The strength of innocence is felt though not intellectually grasped. So in the story of the loss of Paradise one can indicate in a childlike way that sin is the loss of innocence, and that "naughtiness" is often a wrong thought about something right in itself. A child can understand that a baby pays no attention to its nakedness and that this is true goodness. This point was brought out because it is a good foundation for handling the usual childish "naughty" stories. The children discussed Adam and Eve's sin in disobeying God with a serious sweetness which was quite touching. They felt truly sad about their losing their Paradise home, where man and animal lived together in peace and love. One child ended the story this way with a little addition of her own—"God went to the serpent and said, 'Hath you made Adam and Eve eat from the Tree of Good and Evil?' The serpent said nothing. God said 'The human beings shall step on the serpent and the serpent will creep up on them and sting them.'"

The story brought another difficult question to the teacher which reminded her of her own childhood. "Why did God like

Abel's present better?" the children demanded. The answer that the fruits of the earth were a better gift at that time, satisfied them and they went happily on to draw dramatic pictures of Cain, surrounded by a thunder cloud, killing Abel haloed in light. This dramatic sense in children can not be considered "bloodthirsty," because they have no adult consciousness of the meaning of murder, or even death. At the same time they knew that another sin had come into the world. As a small girl expressed it "'You killed Abel. This is the worst sin that anybody has done on earth. You will be very unhappy,' God said, and Cain was always unhappy."

The Flood was the climax of this sequence of Bible stories. It took the children's unaccustomed little fingers a long time to write this story down. No difficult questions arose for the teacher from this particular story. The children understood that the people of the earth had forgotten "The Garden of Goodness" and so "One day God felt very sorry that he had created man. God said, "Nobody loves Me", so He made a flood and only Noah and Ham and Shem and Japheth loved God and were saved to see God's rainbow in the sky." The thought of the familiar rainbow reassured the children that never again could such a flood come upon the earth.

This first "epoch" of Bible stories lasted about a month and completed that period in which a child lives in the "Once upon a time". These stories now sink down into the inner life of the children as the next epoch of work begins with the prosaic title "Houses". However, this leads naturally out of the Bible stories, for man's first house on earth is his own body. A brief picture is given of cave houses and then tent dwellers and American Indians.

This will bring us again to the Bible stories. These will be related to tent dwellers and herders for we will start with the story of Abraham and his wanderings—the beginning of history as we know it today.

(1947)   Margaret Peckham

Man and Animal

As Taught in the First Four Grades

This title standing alone will convey little to one not yet acquainted with Rudolf Steiner's pedagogy. One might expect the animal kingdom to be studied in a course by itself, but, as in the world all things are related to each other, we feel that in school, where we are fitting children to live in this world, we must not let them lose sight of the whole while studying details. For this reason we start each course by relating the particular subject to a larger whole. The reasons for relating animals to human beings will be indicated in the following pages.

To the children starting their fourth year at school the title "Man and Animal" is one of delightful significance as a goal finally reached. The first steps leading upward to this goal are taken unconsciously in the first grade when the children listen to fairy stories. On the very first day of "real" school, the small first-graders listen trustingly to the teacher as they are told that they are to begin to learn those things which grown people know and do in the big world. As we talk to these six and seven year old children, we see that their eagerly parted lips reveal half-formed second teeth, or toothless gaps, indicating that the hardest, most material part of their organism is not yet quite finished, and that for this reason they still live to a certain extent in the dreamy, fairytale world of their kindergarten days.

Now, in these tales there are many animals, with animal natures which are just as important to the children as the human characters and, for them, are not really differentiated from the world of man. In the story of *Snow-White and Rose-Red*, for instance, the children love the kind bear, who, not strangely at all, is a prince; or in the tale of *The Golden Bird* they expect the fox to be a friend and guide to the youngest son; and I am sure that no one can feel that the cruel wolf in *Red Riding-Hood* is not an important character. Thus the animals become a living part of the child's world at this age.

As the first year draws to a close, the teacher grows more and more aware of an unfolding and widening of the children's interests and powers of comprehension. After the summer vacation they return to the school definitely more grown-up and alert. The love of fairy stories has not yet vanished, but the teacher can feel that the transition to Aesop's Fables, suggested in the curriculum, is now possible and actually required by their developing consciousness. It is an accepted fact that the fables are a part of the cultural heritage of humanity, yet it is not so clearly realized that they are needed at just this stage of a child's development. The teacher must now use them with care as the perfect food for the child's growing appetite for learning. It is not the right approach to tell a fable and then analyze it in a tiresomely dry and intellectual way. Instead, the appetite is first stimulated by a thorough, pictorial description of people, animals and their ways, all in connection with the particular fable; then, as a climax, one might almost say "dessert", the fable itself is told with its brief and witty characterizations. Now, with their interest thoroughly aroused and thoughts active, sometimes even stirred further by acting out the fable, the children are ready to do some very childlike analysis of their own. Such analysis is based on observation and comparison, as science is. And here it is good for them to describe consciously the difference between the woolly covering of the innocent lamb and the shaggy hide of the wolf, between the cruel, meat-tearing teeth of the wolf and the grass-munching ones of the lamb. These animals are so different, yet they both move parallel with the earth, have four supporting legs and feet, a tail, etc. Such observations can be made at this time when the quality of dreaming is gradually falling away like a cloak, and the animals are no longer looked upon as being just the same as human beings and thus too close to be studied objectively.

140

The next step in preparation for a conscious understanding of the animals comes in the third grade with the study of farming and the farm animals in their relation to the earth and to man, as his willing servants. The children are now two steps removed from fairy-tale dreams, and are ready to feel a conscious love and gratitude toward the animals, who not only serve them but are also dependent upon them. These steps, which are only visible to the teacher, finally bring them to the fourth year and its goal.

Having heard many hints from older children in the school about the importance and interest of the study of "Man and Animal", the children are now full of wonder and anticipation, with an eagerness to begin to learn, which proves the truth of Aristotle's saying that "wonder implies the desire to learn". The teacher, who has spent a thoroughly enjoyable and stimulating period of study, preparing the best possible presentation of the subject, is guided by the school curriculum, which says, "first an elementary study of man will be presented to the child in an artistic and reverent manner and then the animal world will be observed, always in its particular relation to man. In this way one teaches the child to perceive the manifold variations of the animal world, and to see how these are united in fixed order and harmony in human beings."

Each teacher who has taught this period of "Man and Animal" stands ready to help the next teacher whose class reaches the fourth grade; but no two teachers approach the subject in just the same way, though the fundamentals are of course the same. To this year's fourth grade teacher, it seemed good to relate the first lesson to the Bible stories taught during the previous year. We talked over the stories of Creation, and I recalled to the children the verse which says, "And God said, Let us make man in our image, after our likeness, and let him have dominion over the fish of the sea, and over the fowl of the air, and over the cattle, and over all the earth, and over every creeping thing that creepeth upon the earth". In this way out of their earlier experience, it was natural to the children to start with the idea of the dignity of man made in God's image, which does not imply any concrete physical picture, but rather a sense of the moral character of man, which distinguishes him from the beasts.

Continuing to develop the curriculum plan of presenting man in "an artistic and reverent manner" in order to reveal in him "the variations of the animal world in fixed order and harmony", I turned to a book on zoology which definitely presents man's qualifications as exercising dominion over the animal world, due to certain potentialities. First it points out that we ought "to define the hand as belonging exclusively to man" and continues, "There is in him, what we observe in none of the Mammalia that approach him in other respects,—a complete distinction between the functions of his two pairs of extremities; the upper being adapted to prehension alone, the lower to support only." This naturally leads to "man is further distinguished from all other animals by his erect attitude." The zoologist also emphasizes that man's slow growth and dependence upon parents is "closely connected with his ultimate superiority". And he concludes with two important statements; one, that man's power to "articulate sounds, or language" is another of man's unique abilities, the other, that "above all, it would seem that the mind of man is distinguished from theirs (animals) by the faculty of conceiving of a Superior Being, enjoying a purely spiritual existence". Implied in this last statement is man's moral character which enables him to distinguish between good and evil. These indications, and much more physiological data, were studied by the teacher and presented in a manner suited to nine-year-old children.

Human spiritual superiority to animals having been thus indicated, we can now point out our physical inferiority by showing that in each type of animal some physical part of the organism is carried very close to perfection, though at the expense of other advances in development. It is easy to show the superiority in speed of the horse's one-toed hoof over our delicate foot; or how much better adapted a lion's unsheathed claws are for rending food, than our delicate fingers; and when it comes to the air it is obvious that the eagle's wings outstrip all our limbs in flying. But here we turn back once more to man's superiority, for all that he lacks physically is made up by his potential capacities that work through his creative and imaginative thought. He invents all manner of vehicles which produce great speed, all kinds of tools for cutting and for eating food, and his airplanes of the present and future carry not one, but many through the air.

Having thus introduced man as a whole, the teacher goes on to lessons dealing with our various physiological aspects, among them those which can be experienced directly by the children. The senses now become of conscious interest to them when they realize how unconnected with the world our head might really be were it not for these doors and windows through which we go out to the world and let it in. Compressing their own ribs with their hands and then feeling how the air pushes them out again; letting the air in through the nose and out through the mouth while speaking; feeling the throbbing pulse; observing the color of veins; and recalling the red of arterial blood often seen; all such observations make these daily occurrences a stimulating study. Digestion may also be followed in a simple fashion from experience. With this foundation, the study advances to a comparison of our functions with those of the animals.

To the surprised interest of the children, our head is shown as having its counterpart in such primitive creatures as squids and octopuses, (cephalopoda), whose outreaching tentacles do the work done by our senses. As a simple example of a counterpart of the human trunk in the animal world, we chose the mouse which the children were able to study at first hand, as a pair of white mice live in our classroom. In these tiny creatures one is aware of a short body carried swiftly and lightly by slim legs and feet. At one end the pointed head is attached to supply the body with food and to protect it from danger with the bright watchful eyes, the keen smelling nose, the shell-like, alert ears and the sensitive whiskers. At the other end the long tail serves the trunk by helping to balance it like a fifth leg when the small creature reaches up for a berry on a vine, or cake on a shelf. But when we come to the human limbs, we can find no representative for them in the animal world, for our limbs with their divided duties are unique. This brought us to the end of our first period of the study of animals in relation to man.

When the fourth grade later resumed this study of "Man and Animal" in a second period, their interest and enthusiasm were unabated throughout a brief oral review. Now began a closer and more exact study of the physical characteristics of various groups of animals, starting in the ocean with the cephalopoda. These spineless feeler-equipped creatures were followed in the course of development by fish which breathe through gills, like the goldfish in the bowl on our shelf, and have spinal bones like those which we can observe on our plates after fish dinners. The next surprise came to the children when they learned that a whale is not a fish, but a warm-blooded mammal, "loving" its young, not cold-bloodedly deserting its eggs to hatch and be devoured wholesale. Another surprise was the fact that mother whales nurse their "calves" with milk. One little girl looked at the picture of a whale with its great ugly mouth and remarked disappointedly, "She doesn't look like a mother!" Though some individual animals were studied thoroughly, only a general survey of the animal kingdom is made in the fourth year, giving a foundation for later studies.

Thus we continued our survey and stepped ashore to find other mammals, among whom we visited some small familiar rodents in field and wood, particularly the beavers as they cut down trees without saws and engineered their dams to protect their well-made houses. One child wrote in her book, "beavers have lovely homes". And the same child, with great naivete, ended her description by writing, "beavers are relations of whales". When she read this aloud her classmates were greatly entertained and one said, with a twinkle in her eye, "Perhaps they are cousins because they are both mammals."

To round out the course, we ended with a study of ruminants, especially the cow; the cat family, centering on the lion, the King of the Beasts; and the eagle, as King of the Birds.

This fourth year course about animals in their relation to man lays the foundation for a more mature study of zoology in a higher class. It is on a childlike level, yet has a depth of meaning which forms a true basis for future learning. It wakens in the children an energetic interest for further knowledge and gives them accurate information in an artistic and living way.

(1952)   William Harrer

Work with Underprivileged Children

A Busman's Holiday for a Waldorf Teacher

It began with a conversation at the dinner-table, where a guidance counsellor and a Waldorf teacher had just met. The theme was education, its goals and methods. "Why don't children want to learn?" This weighed heavily on the counsellor's mind. No, she had never heard about Rudolf Steiner's educational ideas. She noted that they were very different from what she was experiencing daily in her school. Were they suitable only for the privileged few in private schools, or would they work also for children from the shadow side of life? . . . A few weeks later she persuaded me, the Waldorf teacher, to try teaching in a school for children from broken homes. I agreed to fill a vacant position until a permanent teacher could be found. It proved to be a twelve-week expedition into the world of the underprivileged child. The equipment I brought was my years of training and experience in Steiner (or Waldorf) education. The age of my charges ranged from ten to twelve.

The Scene

"I hate teachers!" "I hate women!" were the welcoming remarks. The atmosphere was filled with hostility. No, they did not want to read. No, they hated arithmetic! Animosity permeated their own relationships to each other. Fistfights and resulting bedlam could break out any moment. When they were finally talked into writing, the first difficulty encountered would call forth: "I quit!" They would tear up the paper, throw it across the room, and sulk. Assertion of authority was hopeless: "Make me!" was the arrogant reply. Once I dared to point out, matter-of-factly, an arithmetic mistake. The girl flew into a rage: "YOU are wrong. YOU are wrong. You are persecuting me!" . . . It was total rejection. How could I win their confidence?

The First Attempt

"These children are realists" had been the warning of the guidance counsellor. "They have experience, and they know life." Was she right?

A sure way to establish contact with children is to tell stories, and to tell them well, with inner participation and dramatic expression. Children of all ages love good stories. Would this group listen?

Booker T. Washington's autobiography, *Up From Slavery*, was my first attempt. I had just read it again, deeply moved by its humanity. What was their reaction to his childhood experiences? They listened quite attentively. Were they moved? No, they were amused. They laughed, made jokes, found it terribly funny. They thought it silly that he yearned to learn to read. At the age of eight his mother gave him his very first book, a speller, bought with painfully saved money. "You mean that's all he got for Christmas, a book?" His longing to go to school, the almost insurmountable difficulties and hardships evoked jokes: "What does he want to go to school for?"—"I hate school!" etc. . . . They could not identify either with genuine poverty and hardships or with longing for knowledge. Human striving was beyond their sphere of experience and therefore funny. . . . What could reach them?

The First Human Contact

It was at the end of a long school day. Antipathy and disinterest had been expressed freely toward every subject and activity. The skills were limited. Still forty-five minutes to go. My exhausted mind reached for a dramatic Russian legend for younger children, "The Beggar in Paradise." As long as I live, I shall never forget the change that occurred: the eyes grew wide with wonder, their faces relaxed. They literally drank in this beautiful tale . . . My 'realists' would accept the pictorial idealism of mythology.

Homer's *Odyssey*

Greek mythology as story-telling content is Rudolf Steiner's suggestion for this age group. And it was especially the *Odyssey*, told dramatically and in great detail for an hour each day, that helped to remove some of the barriers of hostility, made human communication possible, and established my position as class teacher. I bribed them! I would tell the story for one hour: they in turn would do their work afterwards. The plan for the day was agreed upon and written out on the blackboard. Everyone promised to stick to the agreement.

Habits of years are difficult to break. "I promise" was still an empty phrase. "I don't care," "I quit," on encountering a difficulty, did not cease. Admonishing or moralizing is practically useless. Far more powerful is a dramatic experience in story form where the emotional life gets involved. The perfect example of broken promises and the dire consequences was provided by *Odysseus' Companions*. They had sworn not to touch the cattle of the Sun God. Their light-hearted, I-don't-care attitude was portrayed dramatically, using classroom language without making it too obvious. My listeners smiled; but some grew pale, when later on Zeus bore down on the Companions with thunder and lightning and destroyed each and every one of them. From that time on, "I promise" took on more meaning, and any attempt by one or the other to take it lightly was not tolerated by the rest of the class.

Another big problem was the tone in the class, the crudeness of language, the name-calling. Here the episode of *the Cyclops* worked therapeutically. In his rudeness, the Cyclops was using the crude sounds of classroom jargon. This was contrasted with the friendliness, the openness, and trust of the Greeks, who called him a *Brute*. My students disliked him vehemently and took sides with the Greeks. From that time on, 'Brute' was taken up into classroom lingo. It was frequently used by students as a reproach against anyone who would behave like the Cyclops . . . The tone began to change.

Elementary courtesy had still to be acquired. How do you communicate in a friendly way? How do you speak when you are in trouble? When you need help? *The Shipwrecked Odysseus* taught the lesson. His garments torn, unkempt, ragged, he met the noble princess Nausicaa. First her horror at his looks. But when he opened his mouth and spoke softly: "Please would you help me?" her pride and fear vanished. "You look like a beggar, but your courteous speech tells me that you are a nobleman." . . . Next day the librarian sought me out to tell me that one of my roughest boys had addressed her, "Please, would you help me," in asking for a library book. Courtesy became a serious classroom game.

Many other episodes could be told to illustrate the moral power of good stories, well told. For me, their greatest impact was shown later on during the myth of *Jason and the Golden Fleece*. All the heroes were gathered in the good ship Argo. Lots of hardships had already been weathered. More were to come. Jason stopped the boat before the last, most dangerous, most burdensome trial. He gave a realistic picture of the troubles and hardships ahead of them, then offered a choice: "If any one of you wants to quit, then do it now . . . " At this dramatic and tense moment, one of my worst quitters of the past stood up, stretched out his fist and exclaimed triumphantly: "Oh, *not one* of them is going to quit!"

Some Classroom Activities

The dislike of *Arithmetic* was hard to overcome. Each student had a textbook and was supposed to work at his own speed. This might be reasonable for industrious and eager students—but these students worked with no speed at all! Some could not read the directions, some did not want to work and sulked, some did not care and wrote down as answers any numbers that came to mind. One bright fellow, unskilled with numbers, wrote simply 1 for the first answer, 2 for the second, 3 for the third, etc. Others who worked grudgingly were confused and were lacking in basic skills. There were no right answers! . . . In order to like a subject, you have to meet with some success. We put the textbooks on a shelf. Vigorous number work was taken up as a daily activity, first orally for approximately 45 minutes, then every student working on his own for another period using the material we had just practiced. Colored pencils helped as incentive for careful work. A few weeks later, math had become a favorite subject. Students who formerly would do hardly any work now labored in complete absorption. To get every given problem right was the goal. They would not be satisfied with a mark less than 100—and their offer to do it all over again when a mistake had occurred was accepted. After all, the goal was motivation, the will to finish a given task and to do it well.

With *Reading* the situation was similar. Except for a very few, no one cared. Some could hardly read, most could not pronounce many of the words encountered, did not know their meaning, did not bother to look them up.

With colored chalk, using different colors for dialogue, I wrote poetry on the blackboard—dramatic poems that could be acted out. We read them in chorus and singly, learned to pronounce unfamiliar words, entered into their meaning. They loved it and vied for their turns. There was drama in the room, action and vigor, and improvement of speech habits. At a morning assembly they recited poetry for the school.

Art: A school day is long; the afternoons can get terribly dull if only mental work is on the program. We illustrated events of the Odyssey in crayons and colored pencils. Most students had never done any work of this kind before. Several showed genuine talent. We also retold the stories, sometimes in writing. After all, they were eventful and there was no lack of material. A big success was some practice in geometric drawing, which I introduced with the use of a simple compass and ruler. The division of a circle by 6, 8, 12, 16, etc. fascinated them. They worked painstakingly, using colored pencils to bring out the star-shapes and to create objects of beauty.—It was Christmas time and we sang in class together daily. Some children had beautiful singing voices and even volunteered as soloists. The "Twelve Days of Christmas" was their favorite.

Social Atmosphere

Instead of everyone doing his own thing, I encouraged them to help each other. Halfway good readers became my assistants and would tutor others regularly. They in turn received help in Math from a Spanish boy who turned out to be brilliant in this subject, although his test scores were very low because he could not read. In helping each other, they overcame to a large degree the animosities that were festering. Encouragement had to be given continuously. The 'assistants' were praised highly for every success of their charges.

Some Comments

. . . A new art teacher, who had this group once a week for 45 minutes, showed me their art work with the gratifying but erroneous remark that this was a selected, courteous, and cooperative group, while other teachers had to cope with difficult children.

... James, who up till now had been spending most of his school years in the halls or in the principal's office, and whose former teacher had declared him unteachable, once met the principal in the hall. He went up to him with the statement, "Dr. X., you haven't seen me in your office for a long time, have you?" The principal called him in and inquired what had happened to him. Why, after all the former difficulties, would he now work for this one teacher? "She tells such interesting stories," was one comment, the other, "I love to learn from her, but I hate to have to learn from a book."

... On the last day, Toni, the former woman-hater, shyly made a beautiful card. It read, "Good-bye to the nicest teacher I've ever had." The compliment was accepted as a tribute to the educational ideas, to the teaching methods that worked.

Epilogue

A one-hour documentary film, called "The Way It Is," on the plight of the city school was shown two years ago over educational television. It received nation-wide attention. A second showing, half a year later, was followed by a two-hour dialogue between leading educators of the East Coast area. Then a hard diagnosis was made: the present curriculum is irrelevant, today's teaching methods don't reach the child, don't stimulate his interests, don't channel his energies. The call was made for "new methods, new insights, new ways to read and to reach the child."

The new methods, the new insights, the new ways to read and to reach the child do exist! And it is the tragedy of our time that while every new educational theory is given the headlines, heavily funded, experimented with and eventually discarded, Rudolf Steiner's educational methods are practically unknown in this country.

Why is the search always toward easier absorption of crude information, better and more materials, and now the latest cry: ever earlier beginning of intellectual learning? Is it not always in the direction of greater impersonalization of the learning process, thus ever widening the gulf between the generations?

Rudolf Steiner points in the opposite direction. He calls for the humanizing of the learning process with a minimum of selected materials. He starts with reorientation in the training of teachers. The teacher is to become an artist who works with the most pliable of all art materials, the growing child! Poetry, stories, literature, art, music are to be transmitted in an atmosphere of sympathy by a teacher with capacities, one who lives in these elements. The result is an education of the emotional life, and of motivation, as well as of the mind.

The hope of society in the decades past has been education. But now we are not sure. It is evidently the *kind* of education that is the crux. Bruno Bettelheim, the psychiatrist, has formulated this only too well in speaking of the noisy leaders of the radical left: "Intellect was developed at much too early an age, and at the expense of their emotional development. Although exceedingly bright, some remained emotionally fixated at the age of the temper tantrum." (*Time*, Sept. 5, 1969)

Lest this be the fate of our future, what we need is a learning process that establishes a firm basis of emotion and character on which to build a healthy intellectual life.

(1970)   Gisela Thomas O'Neil

The Perfection of the Human Hand
Lies in its Imperfection

The way a class teacher asks questions reveals the quality of his teaching methods. He may, for instance, put many questions only in order to get the children to repeat their lesson. How boring for them if this happens every day!—then he can experience how a wall of enmity goes up between them and himself. Or perhaps he avoids questions and simply delivers the subject matter, even by reading it from a textbook. Then a sort of No-man's-land stretches out between him and the children, and he can hardly take in what is going on on the other side. No, to get a real working spirit together, one has to bring about an exchange of ideas. One can do this through questions that arouse the children, that start them searching. A good question can set loose a whirlwind of liveliness; it can also produce a reflective musing; it is sure to bring into a child's consciousness something that up to now was merely a dream within him, something he could hardly have expressed in words.

A teacher who has been industrious in working up his material so that he has complete control over it, can approach his subject from all sides and make the most varied excursions out from it. He can safely throw problems out to his class and he need not shy away from anything unplanned: the children will also put questions and expect answers! Instead of stuffing ready-made conclusions and definitions into their heads, he will strive in lively discussions with them to find concepts which call upon the thinking and the feeling and the will of each child.

I would like to give an example of the way we can discover living, flexible concepts in company with the children. But first let us see what Goethe had to say about method as such: "I always wait until I find the *pregnant idea* from which many things can be derived, or rather, one that of itself brings forth spontaneously many things to me; then I am careful to receive them with open mind and with caution."*

The study of the human hand** in comparison with the forelimbs of animals: this shall be our 'pregnant idea' and we shall see it 'bring forth many things.' Let us try to get at them, together with the children, 'with open mind and with caution.'

In connection with any subject matter, for instance starting from the form of the human body, the teacher might show how the human hand presents itself as something highly perfect when compared to the forelimbs of animals. The children will enthusiastically agree with this and will bring forward plenty of facts to support the assertion that we human beings are surrounded by the most varied works of our hands which could never have been made by the animals. One could have the children write a composition on the subject, taken just so far. Then on the following day after a short review of yesterday's discussion, one will surprise them by throwing them the question: "But what do you suppose the animals would say if they had heard us humans yesterday, making all those proud remarks?" And then if hands don't go up right away one can introduce a little scene of conversation and let the children carry it further. There could be quite a bit of drama developed during this study.

The lion speaks: "I have clawing paws that, when I spring, can kill my prey and tear him to pieces. And you, little man, how weak your hands are!" "Man" may try to defend himself, but the eagle interrupts and says: "My wings carry me high into the sunfilled sky, where I am king. But you, remember what happened to Icarus!" And then the fish speaks, and the bee, the beaver, mole, horse, and others: each one shows

* Goethe, *Writings on Natural Science*, 4 vols., edited by Rudolf Steiner, Kuerschner. See R. Steiner *Goethean Science*, Mercury Press, N. Y.
** The stimulus for this study came from the book *Man and Animal*, by Hermann Poppelbaum, Anthrop. Publishing Co., London

his particular superiority so clearly that at first no argument seems possible.

Now one lets the children look at their own hands and one asks: "What is it that is lacking in your hand so that it does not become a claw, a wing, a fin, a hoof, or a shovel-paw?" One should introduce at this point some very detailed descriptions. The children will want to help do this; one can gradually draw out even more by questioning; and finally one can complete the separate pictures. Now one tries to have the children see the one-sidedness of the animals' limbs. For instance, one may ask: "Can the eagle swim with his wings? Can the mole fly with his shovel-paws?" And they will realize that an animal has but one skill only, and for this one particular skill it is fitted out in the most practical way. The fin is a complete oar and therefore cannot be a flier. The wing is all flier and therefore cannot be a runner. The hoof is all runner and therefore cannot be a flier. And so forth.

One can say: "What would happen if the animal were given a human hand?" "It would not be able to live." Now the children will understand that the animal by this entirely one-sided development of its forelimbs has been equipped for "the struggle for existence," to be able to repulse its enemy, to find its food, to maintain its life and the life of its offspring. These observations will be enough for the children for one day if one has done a thorough job, and one can end the lesson with a picture of the magnificent and purposeful perfection but at the same time the obvious one-sidedness of the animal's limbs.

The next day, after the main outlines of this picture have once more been drawn, preferably by the children themselves, one can bring the human hand itself into the foreground, especially in comparison to the animal's forelimbs. And by further questioning one can bring out the fact that the hand is by no means a magnificent bodily tool for some specific purpose, that actually it is not built for any single task. Is it a tool at all, as the fin is, or the wing, or the paw? Obviously not. One will lead the children now to the idea that the human hand is by comparison something altogether unfinished, undeveloped, that it is, so to say, only a starting point for the tool-like limbs of the animals. It *could* have become any one of these, but luckily it did not—for it still keeps the capacity to evolve in all directions. Wherever there is a human hand, there is also human intelligence and reasoning; these faculties invent the tools which the hand needs, which the hand itself is not. The children will now be astonished to see that man actually completes his "unfinished" hand: as fin, for instance, by making an oar, as wing, by making the wing of an airplane. It is apparent that we sometimes need highly complicated machinery manipulated by our hands, to replace the animals' tools.

One cannot emphasize enough the importance of this picture: the hand in the center, surrounded by extreme, one-sided forms evolved for definite purposes—as one finds them in the limbs of animals. Rather than a sharply defined picture, there should be lively, imaginative images that show forms in constant metamorphosis as the harmonious human hand changes into the special, exaggerated, one-sided, unbalanced limb of the animal.

And one presents a second picture: of the hand forgoing all these metamorphoses and instead making its own tools.

Such living, imaginative pictures allow the idea of *human freedom* to take root in the children's souls: human freedom which bursts the fetters in which the animal must remain. For the animal has no choice; it lives as its organism prescribes. "The animal must and people can," is how the children have expressed it.

For why is it that if the animal had human hands it would fail in its struggle for existence? The children will discover that it will fail because it lacks the human reasoning which alone would enable it to make free use of the various possibilities our hand offers us. We as well as animals have to undergo the struggle for existence. But while the animal spends its entire life in this struggle, our real life begins when we get beyond the struggle and become creative. Our hands are not chained to the earth, thanks to the upright position of our body; they are free. That is why we can and should change the earth, and make full use of the creative capacities within our hands to develop a culture—as farmer, artist, engineer, laborer, writer. And the children should become fully aware of the wide manual activities by which the human being masters his earth-task. Although one can call the forelimb a tool of the animal's body, one has had to reject this term for the human hand; now however one can use it in a new sense, in that one recognizes the hand as *a tool of the human spirit*.

Once more the children should study their hands and feel how wonderful they are in their detailed structure, their versatility, agility, flexibility. How much a hand can learn! We discuss the ability of a fine mechanic, a violinist, a surgeon, a juggler. How strange that no single hand is exactly like another! That could not be said of the horse's hoof or of the fin of a fish. Think also how our hand clasps another person's hand in greeting; what healing forces can go out from a hand; how the hand of an old man can give a blessing; how, when we fold our hands in prayer, the forces which otherwise go out actively are held back and turned inward. This is a world far away from the animals' world. The fact is apparent even in human speech; when we speak of thinking, which belongs only to man of all the kingdoms of nature, we have expressions that relate to the conscious use of our hands: for instance, we touch a subject, we handle a problem, we grasp an idea, we hold on to it.

That the hand is altogether *a tool of the human spirit*: this is the understanding the children should carry home with them at the end of the third day. Having reached this high point in the discussion one could bring it to a close.

However, this fruitful theme could call forth many more questions. We will just suggest a study that could be made later, perhaps even in a religion lesson. If one has the children look again at the things they are able to create and do with their hands, not leaving the world unchanged but everywhere imprinting the marks of their activity upon it, then some child is likely to observe that hands can also work destructively—for instance, in robbing the soil until vast land-areas are laid bare. Wherever forces of the human spirit are active, there the opposing forces rise up also. And the children can begin to ponder not only the fact that there *is* evil in the world, but *why* it is there. From this point the discussion could go in many directions.

Such thoughts as these can be given to children of the sixth or seventh grade. What here may seem far too tightly woven will become, in the actual teaching, stretched much wider, and therefore will be simpler for the children to understand. The logical condensation here should there become a meaningful series of imaginative pictures, which lead to the sort of conclusions a twelve- or thirteen-year-old child can grasp. The thoughts evolved in this way will have no hard contours; they will be living, flexible, formative, so that later they can be broadened or transformed by new ideas, new points of view. For the 'pregnant idea', from which we started, suggests so much 'spontaneously', that we will constantly be hitting upon it in later studies and led thus into ever new directions.

Whoever puts questions later on to one of these children about the ideas we have worked our way through, must not expect to receive automatic, fixed answers. The child will have to recreate in his own mind the sequence of thought which brought us to the end result. If he can do this in his own way, the goal of our pedagogy will have been reached. For it is a question of the *way* he will have thought the thing through, not alone the conclusion he will reach. The latter could have been given him logically as a concise definition— and how much simpler it would be then to question him! This indeed would correspond more exactly to today's intellectual practices, which must be rejected by a truly creative pedagogy.

A discussion such as we have tried to describe leads right into the sphere of moral and spiritual values. It is improbable that a child growing up with ideas of this nature could ever succumb later on to a materialistic conception of man, with all its dire consequences.

(1962)   Martha Haebler

(Translated by Clara von Woedtke and Gladys Hahn)

Now it always fills me with horror to see a teacher standing in his class with a book in his hand teaching out of the book or the notebook in which he has noted down the questions he wants to ask the children and to which he keeps referring. The child does not appear to notice this with his upper consciousness, it is true, but if you are aware of these things then you will see that the children have a subconscious wisdom and say to themselves: He does not himself know what I am supposed to be learning. Why should I learn what he does not know? This is always the judgment that is passed by the subconscious nature of children who are taught by their teacher out of the book.

Rudolf Steiner
The Kingdom of Childhood

Multiplication Tables Can Be Interesting

Mastery of the multiplication tables is an indispensable tool for the student of arithmetic. Unfortunately, the learning of the tables is often a drudgery for the child and for this reason is frequently the cause of a deep and lasting dislike for everything dealing with mathematics. While it is easy for some children to memorize the tables, it is very hard work for others. Why does an adult know that 7x8=56, with the same certainty that a child knows 2x2=4? It is simple to visualize 2x2=4, but it is much harder to follow consciously the process involved in the multiplication 7x8. However, it would be time wasted if every time we multiply 7x8 we had to go through a conscious process of visualization. We are so sure of the correct answer because long experience has traced it into our memory. It is also through manifold experiences that the child gradually will be able to conquer the tables.

Memorizing the tables abstractly is tiresome, especially for those children to whom the world of numbers is yet strange. When the tables are memorized abstractly as one memorizes historical dates divorced of meaning or understanding, the material becomes a burden and usually is forgotten as soon as the memorizing process stops.

There is actually no reason why the learning of tables should be a drudgery to any child. Every mother who observes her child knows of the joyful, untiring activity of counting when he begins to learn his numbers. It is not an accident that so many nursery rhymes deal with numbers and with counting. Keeping alive this natural joy and desire in rhythmical counting is an old and successful method of working with the tables. It has been abandoned by modern educators probably because it has degenerated into a meaningless drill. But in the grades of a Rudolf Steiner school the tables are a part of the arithmetic lessons throughout the elementary department. The most interesting way of reciting the tables can become dull if excessively used without variation. If, however, the teacher succeeds in vitalizing the old method by filling the old basket continuously with new and attractive fruit, the rhythmical recitation of the tables will be the very activity which is whole-heartedly enjoyed by the children.

When the little kindergarten child recites his nursery rhymes, he satisfies a natural desire. When he reaches the grades he can recite the tables and find in them the same sort of natural, satisfying activity; as, for instance, in

> three is *one* times three
> six is *two* times three
> nine is *three* times three, etc.

And when the recitation is accompanied by physical movements it also becomes a pleasurable and effective exercise.

Of the many possible ways of working with the tables, only a few can be mentioned. In practicing the three table, for example, the children walk in a circle, counting 1, 2, 3; 4, 5, 6; - - -; taking one step to each count and clapping their hands with each step. Doing it over again the 3, 6, 9, etc., are more accented than the rest of the numbers, the steps on them are firmer, and the claps louder. Finally after several rounds, the spoken counting of 1, 2, -; 4, 5, -; 7, 8, -, etc., is left out entirely or done silently while the clapping and stepping are rapid and light. Only the 3, 6, 9, . . . etc., are spoken; the movement stops so that the children experience a slight shock as they come to each number in the three table.

In another exercise of the three table one can make use of a eurythmy exercise—the short, short, long rhythm, for instance,—in which two short steps are followed by one long one.

Still another excellent exercise can be used with any one of the tables. Taking, for example, the eight table: the children run swiftly and lightfootedly for eight steps, stop suddenly for a moment and then continue as before, up to 16, then to 24 and so on.

When such exercises are thoroughly enjoyed, the tables do not become a burden in the storage house of the brain. One can say they actually become part of the child because his whole being has been used in the learning process.

Instead of doing these exercises in a circle they can be arranged along the sides of geometrical figures which are, first, drawn on the floor and then just imagined. For the three-table, the basic form is the triangle; for the four-table, the square; for the five-table, the pentagon; etc. This opens up a great wealth of most interesting combinations and possibilities for geometrical forms and transformations. Thus the child not only learns to know the tables, but also becomes intimately acquainted with geometrical forms. This lays the foundation for a natural understanding of geometry in later years.

Working with the tables as described so far, however, only partially completes the work. There is another side which must not be neglected. The mentioned activities make use of the child's will impulses and his desire to express himself rhythmically. In contrast to the very active "doing" of the tables, a more quiet way should also be used to bring about a balance.

The young students are eager to write down what they have learned, especially if it can be arranged in a chart. Here again there are many possibilities, and the children should be encouraged to invent charts of their own. Table charts offer opportunities to practice the tables by appealing to the pupils' reasoning capacity and sense of discovery, thus sharpening and developing these powers.

In the chart opposite (p. 163), the lines of the tables are drawn in such a manner that each table appears only once and yet each line crosses all of the others. The drawing we arrive at is pleasing in its symmetric and harmonious construction. It offers opportunities for many interesting arithmetical exercises, which fascinate the children, and awaken

162

and stimulate their powers of observation. They are very curious and expectant as the teacher draws the lines of the tables on the board—beginning with the one-table and the twelve-table—and each line in a different color. After all lines are drawn the pupils are eager to help place the numbers. They soon discover that there is no crossing of lines for 2x2; 3x3; etc., and we mark these places with special little squares. When they see that all the squares line up in a definite order on the inside of the chart, they are happily surprised. The table for the little squares is new and we name it the "square table". It does not take long until they know it by heart.

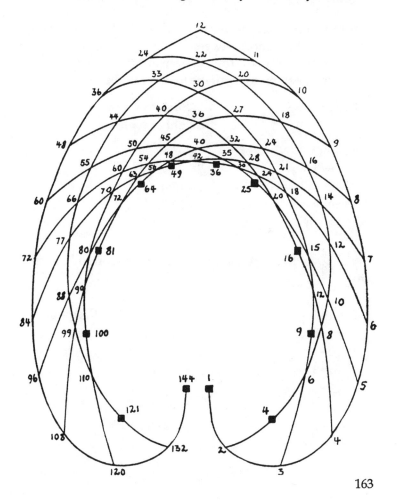

Now continuing our exploration along the chart, one child discovers that the numbers in the middle on the top of the drawing are all even numbers, 42, 40, 36, 30, 22, 12. The adjacent rows of numbers to the right and left alternate, even and uneven:

36, 35, 32, 27, 20, 11
and 49, 48, 45, 40, 33, 24

The row on either side is again even:

30, 28, 24, 18, 10
56, 54, 50, 44, 36

A little hint from the teacher makes the class see that by taking the difference between the numbers in sequential order, we find, in all the rows of even numbers, the following differences, beginning with the lowest number:

Center row—		First even row to right of center—
42-40=2	or	30-28=2 etc.
40-36=4		28-24=4
36-30=6		24-18=6
30-22=8		18-10=8
22-12=10		

In the rows that alternate even and uneven numbers, we have:

Beginning with square right of center		Beginning with square left of center	
36-35=1	or	49-48=1	etc.
35-32=3		48-45=3	
32-27=5		45-40=5	
27-20=7		40-33=7	
20-11=9		33-24=9	

By subtracting the corresponding numbers on the right and left sides of the chart, we obtain the thirteen-table, as follows:

24-11=13	33-20=13	40-27=13
36-10=26	44-18=26	50-24=26
48-9=39	55-16=39	60-21=39
60-8=52	66-14=52	70-18=52
etc.		

By adding corresponding numbers as, for instance, 144+1=145, and 132+2=134, and then subtracting the sums, we always get the same answer provided we follow sequential order. This time we begin at the bottom of the chart.

144+1=145	or	132+2=134
132+2=134		121+4=125
−11		−9
120+3=123		110+6=116
−11		−9
108+4=112		99+8=107
−11		−9
etc.		etc.

These are only a few of the interesting discoveries which the children make by studying this chart. It is not a device for learning the tables because it can hardly be introduced before the fourth grade, when the children should be familiar with the tables at least up to the six-table. Rather, it is a device to show the tables in a new light, which also reveals many interesting relationships between them. Exploring this and other charts helps to make the tables not only interesting but captivating and from these first simple steps the study of mathematics becomes a real experience to the children.

Working with the tables in the indicated manner is never drudgery and never dull. It offers ample opportunity to keep the quick, alert, young mathematicians on their toes and at the same time keeps the slow ones constantly interested and alert.

(1957)   William Harrer

First Lessons in Botany

In a Rudolf Steiner school the first stories about the plants begin in the first grade or even in the kindergarten. But it is not until the fifth year of school life that the children start what they are proud to call Botany. Plant life is now taken up in close relation to the living organism of the earth. The children are made to feel that it is as much a part of the earth as the hair is a part of their heads. The hair by itself is nothing; it cannot grow by itself and has no meaning apart from the human head. Similarly the plant only has a meaning in its relationship to the earth and the forces of the sun. So the flowers may actually be called the children of the sun, growing upon the earth.

First of all a mood of wonder is awakened as one pictures the miracle of the springtime—how from the dead branches of the trees appears the living green like a veil thrown over them; how from the root-stock of a plant is thrust one day a slender sprout which will produce a replica of the plant which died down last autumn; and how from the tiny seed there springs a plant which resembles in every way the mother plant. Whence comes this new life? If we examine the seed, even with the most powerful microscope, we can see nothing that remotely resembles the plant which grows from it. We must conclude that the future plant exists potentially and invisibly within the seed or bulb. And now the children are given a picture of the two polaric forces at work in the plant world; the earth force, tending to draw the roots down to the center of the earth and to harden and give form to the plant; and the sun force, working principally in the leaves, flowers and fruit, tending to draw the plant upwards. The plant becomes ever finer and more ethereal as we go from the root towards the blossom, the perfume of which often extends far beyond the plant itself. This basic concept unlocks many of the secrets of plant life and is woven like a golden thread throughout the course.

166

Children always enjoy a journey—even though it be an imaginary one—so the study may be formed into four journeys: first, a journey through a typical plant from root to blossom; second, a journey from Pole to Equator, viewing the vegetation as the very countenance of the earth; third, the ascent of a high mountain in the tropics; lastly a journey through the plant kingdom itself from the simplest to the most complex plants.

In the first journey we see what each part of the plant can do for the life of the plant as a whole, and the various forms which each part may assume.

In the second journey we have a bird's-eye view of the vegetation from the Pole to the Equator. Near the Pole the sun forces are very weak and the water, which is the very life-blood of the plant, is frozen most of the year. So there is almost a total absence of plant life. The wide stretches of earth are like masses of stone.

As we travel away from the Pole, the sun's heat increases, the water is no longer frozen during the whole year, and we have a scanty vegetation consisting of mosses and lichens. Here the earth force works strongly upon plant life, binding it to the surface like a green carpet.

As we near the Temperate Zone, the sun has more power. Plants have now the strength to rise somewhat away from the earth, but they are still dwarfed and stunted. The fir tree, which grows to such height and beauty in our climate, only creeps along the earth—the trunk like a root from which the branches rise like little bushes. The hardening forces, usually confined to the root, have here spread through the whole plant.

But we must not think that the Arctic regions are without bloom. As soon as the snow melts there is an exuberant growth of flowers of an intense color and matchless purity. Butterflies and bees swarm about them; the seeds develop quickly and fall to the earth, and the plant disappears only to repeat the same miracle over again. It is as if heaven had

sent its loveliest blossoms to this otherwise cold and cheer-
less land

Next we come to the Temperate Regions. Here the sun
rises higher in the sky and the summers are longer. The sun
force increases greatly and plant life becomes more and more
free from the earth's hold. First we meet the evergreens,
which rise majestically to a great height; next come the
deciduous trees with their crowns of green foliage. There is
also an endless variety of flowering plants.

In the Tropics the sun reaches its greatest intensity. Summers are long and very hot. Trees rise like giants from the
earth, climbing vines fling themselves from trunk to trunk,
reaching up for light. Tree trunks and tree crowns shelter
magical gardens overhead. So great is the pull of the sun
force that the earth is no longer able to hold certain plants.
Such is the orchid which has its roots in the air and gets its
nourishment from air, dew and rain. In the Tropics the
flowering tendency is so strong that its power often penetrates to the very heart of the plant, and we have the spice
plants with their aromatic roots, bark and leaves.

So we can picture the vegetation of the whole earth like
one great plant which has its roots at the Pole, its stem and
leaves in the Temperate Zone, its blossoms and fruit in the
Tropics.

The journey from the Pole to the Equator is repeated in
miniature, but in reverse order when we climb a lofty peak
in the Tropics, for each mountain comprises within itself a
picture of the whole earth. At the base of the mountain we
find the giant trees of the Tropics. The higher we climb the
colder it grows until we reach the trees of our Temperate
Zone where evergreens mingle with the foliage trees. As we
ascend higher the trees become dwarfed and stunted and we
finally reach the "timber line". Next comes the moss-lichen
zone and as we approach the snow-line we stand enraptured
before the masses of lovely blossoms at our feet, perfect
replicas of the Arctic flowers. Last of all we reach the region

of eternal snow and bitter cold, with no sign of vegetation—a veritable Pole in miniature.

And now for our journey through the plant kingdom itself. First let us look at one of the lower plants, the mushroom, which we usually find growing in the deep woods away from the sunlight. The flowers of the higher plants open up towards the heavens and take the sunlight into themselves. But mushrooms open downwards towards the dark earth. They have no blossom and so cannot form seeds, but produce new plants by means of spores. They have no green leaves either, and so cannot make their own food but live on the food that other plants have made. They have not even any roots with which to get a foothold on the solid earth. We might call the mushroom the baby among the plants, for it is as helpless and dependent as an infant. A little school-girl once said, "It is because the mushrooms are babies that so many of them have milk inside them."

Mosses and ferns are a step higher than the mushrooms, for they possess the green substance called chlorophyll, and are not dependent upon other plants for their food. They are not yet able to form flowers, however, but produce spores like the mushrooms. So we may think of the mosses and ferns as being a little older than the babies—the mushrooms—for they are able to make their own food. They also have stems and can stand erect. They are not, however, fully developed plants, since they have no flowers and no real fruits.

Next we come to the evergreen trees, beloved of children for their association with the joys of the Christmas season. Botanists call them *conifers* or cone-bearers. They are the simplest of the plants which produce true seeds instead of spores. They send down strong roots deep into the earth and with their erect stems, or trunks, they reach up towards the sun, often attaining a height of two hundred feet. They produce leaves, flowers and fruit, but all their parts tend to contract and to grow hard. Their leaves are nothing but a midrib; they are well named needles. The blossoms appear but are held back. They look like little curly caterpillars at first, and finally harden into cones. But the forces thus held back in the blossom produce instead an aromatic resin which penetrates the whole tree: wood, bark and cones. The needles also yield an aromatic oil. This, together with the resin, gives the trees their pleasant balsam fragrance. The seeds, with their little wings, are hidden under the scales of the cones, so the cones are both flower and fruit.

In these trees everything moves slowly. Some cannot produce seeds until they are two hundred and fifty years old. The needles stay on the branches for several years and in some species a cone takes several years to ripen. Many evergreens live to be several hundred years old. They seem to possess great inner tranquility. On entering an evergreen forest one is moved by a feeling of great solemnity.

These simplest seed-bearing plants we might compare to the young child before the age of seven—not yet ready to blossom forth into the school age, but fully out of its babyhood.

A step higher in the plant kingdom come the members of the lily family which grow from bulbs or corms. The lilies and grasses are *Monocotyledons*—that is, they have but one seed-leaf. Their leaves are simple in form and parallel-veined. The lilies do not associate so freely with the earth through their roots as do the grasses, but set themselves apart from the earth and make a little world of their own with its own rhythm.

The lily family, coming before the sun's rays have really penetrated the earth, gives us our first spring blossoms. The children like to hear that they can flower so early because they bring their lunch boxes with them, for stored within the bulb is all the food they need for their blooming.

The lily has always been the symbol of innocence and purity. The angel Gabriel, when announcing the birth of the Christ Child, holds a lily. The Madonna and Child are often painted with lilies about them.

If we compare this flower to the human being, we could say that it is like a child at about the age of seven. The child has something almost lily-like at this age and has, so to speak, put forth a lovely, fragrant blossom, but is still quite simple and undeveloped.

The grasses are distinguished from all other flowering plants by their small, inconspicuous flowers. From their tiny blossoms, however comes the seed that gives bread to man, for the grains—corn, wheat, rye, barley, rice and oats—are all members of the grass family. Instead of developing a colorful, showy blossom, the grasses have stored up their life within the seed, as in a little treasure-box. They live very close to Mother Earth—hence their quick growth and sturdiness. It is the mother-milk of earth which we taste in the sweetness of the corn. The grasses have sacrificed their blossoms that they may give food to man, and man may think of this reverently, and reverently partake of his bread as a true gift of the sun and earth.

A Blessing before Meals

Earth, who gave us all this food,
Sun, who made it ripe and good—
Sun and Earth, we pray that ye
Never shall forgotten be.

Christian Morgenstern

Lastly we come to the top rank of the flowering plants, the *Dicotyledons* or plants bearing two seed-leaves. As examples of this very large group let us look at the apple tree and the rose. We may think of a tree trunk as being a portion of the soil itself, drawn upward and encased in bark. So the tree-crown is in reality an assembly of many single plants which sprout overhead in the branches and burst into leaf and blossom earlier than do plants growing out of the ground. This is possible since they grow on the already plantlike living tree trunk instead of in the earthy, mineral soil.

The apple tree is our most important fruit tree, but it is also a flowering tree. Its blossom is very like the wild rose; each has five pink petals and a five-pointed green calyx. But the five-pointed star which the rose blossom carries within itself appears only in the fruit of the apple tree. It can be seen when the apple is cut through crosswise. The apple tree and rose are the parents of a large plant family. The rose, with its lovely blossoms, is the mother; the apple tree, which excels in the formation of its fruit, is the father; while the strawberry is the baby of this plant family.

It is clear at a glance that the apple tree tries to make everything as simple as possible. Its leaves are strong and healthy, but very simple in form, while the rose takes infinite pains with her beautiful, elaborately formed leaves. The apple tree strives above all for fruitfulness, and its fruit is fully penetrated with the juices of the fruitful earth. The rose is an artist; her blossoms have never been excelled for beauty and fragrance. She is well-named the Queen of the flower kingdom.

In our further study of plant life we learn to know many trees: the strong, majestic oak, reaching its full strength and beauty only at a great age; the graceful birch, suggesting sunlight, springtime and youthful freshness; the water-loving willow, which grows quickly but as soon decays; and the noble linden, its blossoms offering a feast of nectar to the bees and a health-giving tea for human beings. So we see that nature strives always "to balance all that is one-sided, and never to let beauty fail."*

Such an elementary study of Botany does not aim to analyze flowers in a technical, scientific way—that belongs to a later age—but to give a key to the understanding of plant life in all parts of the earth and under all conditions. Above all it strives to arouse in the children a feeling for the wonder and beauty of the spring awakening, that they may say with

* Note: The material for this article was gained chiefly from Karl Ege's course on *Plant Life in Autumn* given at the Waldorf School Seminar, Stuttgart, and from Dr. Gerbert Grohmann's books on Botany.

Linnaeus as they witness the opening of a flower: "I saw God in His glory passing by and bowed my head in worship."

(1948)   Virginia Field Birdsall

The faculty of personal judgment is not ripe until the fourteenth or fifteenth year. Only then has the child developed to a point where the teacher is justified in appealing to his faculty of judgment. At the age of fourteen or fifteen the child can reason for himself but before this age we injure him, we retard his development, if we continually enter into the "whys and wherefores". The whole of later life is immeasurably benefitted if, between the seventh and fourteenth years, the child has been able to accept a truth not because he sees its underlying reason but because he feels that the teacher whom he reveres and loves feels it to be true.

Rudolf Steiner

IV

THE WHOLE SCHOOL

In its very nature Steiner's educational philosophy stands in the center of one of the great questions of modern education, the mutual relation of the sciences and the arts . . . The tension between the two worlds shifts its ground but remains unresolved. It can only be properly released when a disciplined artistic perception becomes part of the method of natural science, and when the healthy objectivity of the sciences penetrates those finer feelings on which the life of the humanities finally rests. Such a marriage of the arts and sciences, a marriage in the core of their being, based on the ultimate unity of human experience, is one of the great, essential themes of a Steiner education.

A.C. Harwood
The Recovery of Man in Childhood

Imagination At Different Ages

A small child is entirely—as modern child-psychology would express it—a motor being: a being who lives completely in movement, in doing, who therefore is acting directly out of his will. There is not yet the slightest deliberation by his intelligence. Want, wish, impulse determine his actions. Everyone knows how useless it is to "explain" to him why he should or should not do this or that.

Every act of creation is Will. Even the Old Testament is witness to this fact. It was only *after* God acted that He "saw that it was good." And moreover, not only the creating is Will but also the creation itself—however strange that may seem to be. When a new human being enters this world, the reality of the event is truly described by saying, a newborn child is materialized Will. The child has no capacity but willing, even though the willing is at first only a mirroring, an imitation of his surroundings. Only gradually in this will-being does consciousness arise, and ideation, and thinking. And precisely this awakening of ideation on the child's will-foundation signifies the birth of imagination.

The child's imaginative activity emerges spontaneously; it does not come through any external stimulus. The teacher's task is so to guide this activity that when the child as a young adult has finished school and goes out into the world, he goes prepared to face the demands not only of modern technical life but of all modern life in general.

A human being's imagination undergoes a metamorphosis in the course of a lifetime. If we want to follow its transformations, we must begin by observing its first phase, the small child's spontaneous fancy. When a healthy three-, four-, or five-year-old plays, any bit of rag he picks up is the Princess' gown or Mary's cloak or Cinderella's apron. A chair is a car, a house, a vegetable wagon. The child has his will at his command and also a world of images. These images are called forth primarily by the fairy tales and other stories the child is told by the grownups. They do not come from his perceptions as do the concepts of an adult. For the child it is quite unnecessary ever to have seen a wolf or a princess or a frog; he possesses nonetheless an inner image of wolf and princess and frog—not to mention gnome and fairy and witch. Nor does he need ever to have seen representations of them. External perception—which for an adult is the principal source of his images—is for a child entirely secondary. If a fairy tale has been told clearly and vividly, the child holds in himself the images it has evoked. And he has them to use in his play. So we see will-activity as the base, and crowding up out of it, a wealth of images which the child uses in free creative play.

Then at the change of teeth we see the child's feeling, emotional life begin gradually to establish its independence. In the small child it had been completely bound to his willing, and thereby to his organic processes. Feelings of joy and sorrow, comfort and discomfort, still have an immediate effect upon his digestion, growth and vitality. One can find adults, too, obviously, whose emotional life works deeply into the bodily functions. However, we can now observe that when the child reaches school age, there begins to take place in him an ever-increasing independence of the feeling life. We can even notice that whereas previously the feeling life was directly bound up with the will life, now it gradually connects itself much more strongly with the conceptual thinking. We can see clearly that the child's imagination is no longer entirely dependent upon his willing. The fostering of a rich, diverse feeling life will now give his imagination the nourishment it longs for. True, a healthy, strong will such as is developed by an artistic method of teaching will still provide the base; but now the depth and range of his feeling life will determine whether his imagination is rich or poor.

It would be interesting in this regard to compare the students of a school that prepares them in the traditional way for high school and college or technical school by focusing their entire attention upon "learning", that is, upon acquiring an intellectual grasp of the school subjects—to compare those students with those of a school in which a teacher, full of his subject and full of enthusiasm, is able to give his class a vivid experience of it. Suppose a student writes a report on some subject his class has been studying: if the subject has been presented with the express purpose of preparing the class for examinations, making sure that the subject matter has been properly grasped and thoroughly learned but no more than that, then the average student will certainly be able to write a satisfactory report, but the report will be dry, abstract, unimaginative. But if through a teacher's enthusiasm the subject has been presented in such a way that it has been a lively experience for the class, then the report will be enhanced by an imaginative quality.

And this is related to a remarkable secret, of supreme importance to every elementary and high school teacher. This is the secret: that every single object of study—plant, animal, geographical region, historical period, an aspect of grammar or arithmetic—any and every subject lies imbedded in a far larger whole, is by its nature the center of an entire world. A real teacher, wanting to build his subject into a bright experience for his class, will in his enthusiasm bring in a great deal of material from the periphery of the subject, particularly details which could easily be forgotten later but which at the moment will have a strong impact upon the feeling life of the children sitting there in front of him. The whole subject will come to life for them as their imagination is kindled; they will take it and keep it as a lifelong treasure.

It follows therefore that the personal contact between a teacher and his class can never be replaced by books, written assignments, cable TV or such, no matter how ingenious these may be. Only a teacher's personal relation can enrich a child's feeling life; it alone can broaden and deepen the child's inner life in such a way that the child's imagination grows with the child, becoming ever richer and more powerful.

When the young person reaches his third developmental period, in which critical thinking begins to play a dominant role, the danger arises that his intellect may destroy much that has been built up so carefully. Now it is of the greatest importance that the teacher should know the "secret" we spoke of above, and that he should put it to use. Also it is of prime importance that he should not neglect that part of his instruction that has to do with the *will*: "Now do it yourselves!" "Look it up yourselves!" With respect to the secret, take, for instance, a subject like *iron*: the students must, of course, be made acquainted with its compounds and its affinities with other substances, but they should also be shown the role iron plays in human blood, how it works in us, the importance of iron in the earth's soil, its necessity for vegetation, its role in cosmic phenomena, etc., etc.—and all this not only with respect to the substance itself but also with respect to its forces and movements.

This third period requires that the students be given practice in thinking, and that their insight be broadened. Undoubtedly one of the foremost tasks the teacher has is to see that when a student finishes school, he shall take away with him "a picture of the world": a world-view, however imperfect it may be, nonetheless a view in which the young person knows that he or she belongs as human beings. A picture that forms *a whole*.

At the same time the teacher's work-plan should allow plenty of time for "do-it-yourselves" and "find-out-about-this-yourselves" assignments. In mathematics, for instance, he can exercise his students' thinking, make it more flexible, if he requires them to discover the theorems for themselves, not just memorize them out of the book; moreover if he points out that there must be a relation of one thing to another—for instance, the transition from circle to ellipse, to parabola, to hyperbola—and has the students visualize all this first mentally and only later confirm it by rediscovering these transitions through the properties of the forms.

To sum all this up: In the first period the teacher must watch that he does not suppress the children's spontaneous imagination by premature intellectual measures. Nowadays the tendency is widespread to introduce adult skills in the kindergarten—for instance, reading and writing, exercises for the various senses, cutting, braiding, weaving—where only healthy play belongs, and the telling of genuine folk fairy tales and children's stories.

In the second period the teacher should stimulate the children's healthy imagination by the artistry of his teaching, so that the children are creative in every way. He should present the various subjects in a broad, rich fashion, so as to make them vivid experiences for the children. In this way their feeling life is enriched and deepened.

In the third period he should help his students understand the world by giving them access to a comprehensive structure of ideas and by helping them to relate themselves to it.

If in this way a teacher holds such a transformation of the imagination in his consciousness, then through his teaching he will prepare the young people to meet the demands of the new age and to find a place in its social pattern where they can do fruitful work.

(1976)   I. van Wettum

*(From "*Erziehungskunst*", January/February, 1959. Translated by Gladys Hahn.)*

"Earth, Who Gives To Us . . ."

The other evening a group of friends were discussing the pressing issues facing us in the decades to come. Was it drugs, war and peace, the younger generation, the racial crisis, political corruption, the changing moral standards, or the East-West confrontation which lay at the heart of the matter? Where could education best serve the future generation to lay a moral foundation to face these issues? Most of these problem areas are symptoms of a failure to respect and understand human beings and our relationship to the world around us. Thus, the current concern for ecology directly relates to the heart of the matter. Then Mrs. G.—, a professional educator, who had had many disillusioning years of supporting idealistic causes, turned to us and said, "As a teacher myself, I feel that I have never really gotten to the core of it. I have inward concerns which I want to share with the children. They share my emotional involvement, but somewhere there is still a split between the day-to-day teaching and the hard facts of reality. I feel it's wrong to overemphasize these problems to young children and yet how else do I develop the feeling of responsibility? If ecology is the basic issue, how does Waldorf education deal with it?"

We began by suggesting that it wasn't a matter of drawing the attention of five- and six-year-olds to the amount of hydrocarbons in the air or pollution in the water, but of meeting the child at his particular age with a positive experience of the world. We then discussed the approach of Waldorf education far into the night. What follows are some of the highlights that we could later recall.

The Four Elements and the Four Kingdoms

These two focal points weave in and out of the Waldorf curriculum like musical themes, threading their way through the child's growth and awareness of his world and himself. *The four elements*—earth, water, air and fire—were recognized by the Greeks to be the four "roots" of which the world is composed. They are the active forces working in the world and within us. In chemistry these could be equated to the four states of matter: earth, physical solid substance; water, liquids; air, gases; fire, warmth. *The four kingdoms*—mineral, plant, animal and human—inhabit the earth.

Characterizing the phenomenal world in this way enables the child to grasp the facts of the world clearly. These are dynamic categories which are intellectually true, yet applicable to all ages.

The Early Years—Preschool & Kindergarten

Because the young child lives in imitative activity, it is very important to have an attitude of reverence and love for all the kingdoms of nature. He learns through the will. Many opportunities are presented to actually participate in practical activities. To the young child the world is one; the world is good. He digs the earth, carefully waters the soil or rejoices when the rain does it for him. He sees that the wind in autumn carries the leaves to the ground or spreads the seeds. Father Sun sends his loving warmth to all that lives and grows. The children lovingly care for their garden, harvest the crops, bake bread, gather fruit and delight in the smells that fill their room when they are cooking. The earth to the young child is not just "dirt" but a living home for the seeds, beetles and stones. Plants have a rhythm of their own and children delight in the sprouting and budding of each one. That a giant sunflower can come from a tiny seed is a source of constant awe. There is the excitement of experiencing the earthworm ploughing the earth, the caterpillar changing into a butterfly, the mother cat having her kittens. This can be experienced in the center of a city if we are willing to trade cement for even a very small plot of earth. The teacher is the primary representative of man. It is her inner attitude and outer activity which affects the young child. The teacher

181

must fully enter these activities rather than stand aside. She must be willing to get her hands dirty and feet wet as she explores the world with knowledgeable but awe-filled joy. The class itself is Man—the cooperation, the recognition of differences, the working out of social situations, the times to be alone, the times to come together.

The themes of the four kingdoms and the four elements pervade the stories the children hear and act out. These are active in the fairy tales, in their songs, paintings, beeswax modeling, rhythmic exercises and drawing. A grace before lunch, often used, is:

> *Earth who gives to us this food,*
> *Sun who makes it ripe and good,*
> *Dear Earth, dear Sun, by you we live,*
> *Our loving thanks to you we give.*

First and Second Grades

While many of the same outer activities continue, with the beginning of "formal" schooling more time is spent inside the classroom. Reading, writing and arithmetic are pervaded by the four elements and four kingdoms as expressed in nature and fairy tales. Out of the story of the water cycle can come the "W" (the waves), the "F" (the fish), and the "M" (the mountains), etc. In the second grade, fables and legends, which are teaching tools for reading and writing, carry insights into animals and man. Underlying the educational experiences in these early school years, is *love for the world.* For, without *love*, what is there to conserve?

Conservation or Ecology?

There is a basic difference underlying these two words. *Conservation* implies conserving natural resources for the future. In conservation human beings take an active part protecting (subduing) nature for their own use. Reforestation programs are initiated so that we can all have more lumber in the future; waterways are stocked so that there will be more trout for fishermen. Deer are protected so that hunters may pursue the sport for a longer time.

Ecology is much more subtle. Here it is not for the human being but for all living creatures—for the earth itself. Rather than planting trees or stocking fish as isolated remedies, there must be a consciousness of the great life patterns such as the nitrogen and water cycles, the intricate and delicate *balance* upon which all of the kingdoms are dependent.

Third Grade

During this year the child begins to separate himself from his surroundings. He stands more objectively in relation to his world. In this feeling of loneliness, it is a help to engage in activities that build confidence. Third grade is a very practical year. The Old Testament forms the history-literature theme. After Adam and Eve are sent out from Paradise they must learn to work the earth, to build their home, to form a community. From this comes the study and practice of farming and house-building. The farmer—as human representative—must learn to work the earth, to know and work with the air and water, the weather, and the warmth if he is to have a successful farm. But this is not complete without the four kingdoms. The minerals are needed to enrich the soil or for a stone wall, the plants are needed for food, the trees for shade and for holding the soil. The animals fertilize the earth, help in pollination, carry burdens, pull ploughs, give milk, eggs, meat or wool. The farmer must consider others as he plans his farm—those who send him seeds, repair broken parts for his tools and machines, who pick up surplus milk or deliver extra hay; those who will eat the food or weave the wool or cotton. And so in the end all comes together in one picture—the farmer stands as the balancer amongst the kingdoms and elements—a unity of many.

Fourth, Fifth and Sixth Grades

In these middle grades, the emphasis is not so much on man the balancer and user but on the phenomena themselves. Having gone from the total picture in the early grades, we now move to a more profound study of the individual kingdoms.

In fourth grade the animal kingdom is dramatically portrayed. The children enter into the sensitive relationship existing between each animal and its home. They come to respect the specialization of the animal, such as the ability to fly, dig, climb, run, swim. Man, who can do all these, is adaptable to jungle, desert, and plain. He is not nearly so sensitive to nor dependent upon his immediate environment. Just picture for a minute a kangaroo living in a jungle or an elephant on a desert! Hence, if animals' surroundings are disturbed, their existence is threatened.

In fifth grade there is a thorough study of botany. The relationship is studied between plant life and climate, geography and rhythm of the year. The quality and amount of soil, air, water and warmth are very important to the plant. Then the children consider the kinds of plants which are more connected with the earth, those which are airy and hardly seem to be held down by their roots at all, the plants which do best near or in water, and the plants that open and close with the sun. Each plant in its own time unfolds its full possibilities.

In sixth grade the mineral kingdom is taken up in the context of the earth as a living organism. The great forces, such as mountain building, erosion, volcanic action and earthquakes, are studied. The change of rock from mountain top to sand on the beach, of limestone to marble, of thundering waterfalls to a heavily used, polluted river, of ancient fern forests to diamond—all of these are examples of the powerful forces working in this living earth. The kinds of soil that emerge where there is a predominance of one mineral, too much or too little water, good or poor aeration and the quality of heat absorbed, bring in the importance of the elements. Here, as in the study of all the kingdoms, *time* is important. The time and conditions needed for a perfect crystal to form can be millions of years. The children learn to respect the time needed for a forest to grow or a valley to form of sediment. Man's relationship to the mineral kingdom is studied. What part does he play in erosion, farming methods and forestation?

In these middle school years the feelings are stirred by dramatic presentations. Joy, sorrow, anxiety, relief are all experienced. Without the feelings engaged, ecology is just an intellectual study.

Practical Activities

In all the grades, activities appropriate to the age are possible. Camping trips to bring the city child into direct experience of mountains, forests, deserts and seashore are worth weeks of talk and study. In California this has worked most successfully. Classes do portions of their nature studies on location from fourth grade on. Petitions to save nature areas, clean-up projects, newspaper collections, all are direct, practical applications to *conservation*. Hiking, camping and observing wilderness areas give the experiential picture of *ecology*.

Seventh and Eighth Grades

In the seventh and eighth grades physiology is studied. One might question the relevance of physiology to ecology. But in this study is a culmination of the work of the previous years. We are beings of earth, water, air and fire. What has been studied macrocosmically is now seen microcosmically. Just as one appreciated each of the individual kingdoms outwardly—now the wonder and mystery are brought inward. The basic interdependence is seen of natural world and human beings. An intense study of health and nutrition has ramifications for the individual, for mankind, and for the earth as a whole. If one system of the body is disturbed, it affects the whole balance of the body. Poisons absorbed by the body eventually have an accumulative effect. The circulatory system carries these substances to all parts of the organism. So, too, the effects of an atomic explosion in one part of the world are carried to other parts via the earth's circulatory system (water and air).

World geography taken in these grades, where a detailed comprehensive picture is given of mountains, climatic zones, major rivers, oceans, currents of air, gives the macrocosmic picture of the interrelations of all four elements. A formal course in ecology given in this period would make sense, based on the inner experience of the past years. Without the comprehensive buildup it would be a mere superficial treatment. Needless to say, on the high school level, all that has been presented would be dealt with in a technical and more conscious way.

The Human Image

Right through Waldorf education the human image is central. As potentially moral beings we carry a responsibility for the condition of the earth. As civilized beings we change our environment by our very existence. Therefore we have to carry a consciousness of the effects of our deeds. This relates to the way history is approached in a Waldorf school.

If a child has lived with love and reverence for his teachers, parents, classmates and environment when he was young; if his feelings were stirred in the middle grades so that he felt deeply about the tragedies and joys of others; if his thoughts were raised to clear vision of the interrelationship of all things in the upper grades, then the groundwork is laid for meeting the challenging issues of our time. It will become understandable that we cannot escape our environment through drugs, cannot deprive other human beings of their rights without disturbing the whole of mankind and cannot judge the world in our own image but must learn to respect and observe what is there. This is what we are trying to do in Waldorf education to meet the question of ecology.

* * *

When we finished, Mrs. G. said, "I can see there is much more involved in this education than a superficial treatment of nature study. Can we set up another time to meet?"

(1970)   Betty and Franklin Kane

Choral Recitation

"Why is there so much choral recitation in the Rudolf Steiner School?" parents often ask. "Isn't it rather monotonous? Is it good to sacrifice the individual nuances of a single voice in this way? What do the children gain from it? Isn't it a waste of valuable time in which they should be learning?"

The children should and do, of course, recite individually in the classroom. They all sharpen their tongues on tongue-twisters and fill out their voices and lungs on exercises that have sonorous, rolling vowels. But they need more than this. The ten-year-old boy who still speaks in the high tones of a six-year-old, who does not yet place his heel firmly on the ground and whose thoughts wander off into space, like his voice, needs some individual work. The teacher encourages him to speak with the decisiveness and strength of a king or a general. She tries to get his voice to follow the imperious, downward gesture of command or she may have him stamp his foot as he speaks, for speech tends to follow the line and direction of a physical gesture. She may give him alliterations based on the strong, guttural sounds G and K to recite. As the boy works in this way over a period of time, you may gradually notice a new firmness and confidence begin to take hold of his whole nature. The girl who has a tendency to stutter needs harmonious, rhythmical verse to speak, for the rhythmical quality of her breathing is impaired. She needs, too, the kind of exercises that will help her to breathe out fully before she gasps too quickly for the next breath. The boy with the strident voice and the all-too-ready fists can be led to speak with a more relaxed fullness, to become sensitive to the modulations of his voice and the subtleties of the consonants spoken exactly and clearly in the foremost part of the mouth. Thus, through individual speech work the teacher becomes aware of the way in which each child is related to his speech organism, and the child's speech may be one avenue, and a very important one, for understanding, diagnosing his difficulties and helping his development. By guiding his speech, she is provided with one means of leading him to become more daring or gentler, less heavy and insensitive or more down-to-earth, as the case may be. She can help him to breathe more deeply and freely and to become more harmonious in himself and in relation to the world.

If the pupils spoke only in chorus, minor speech defects might pass unnoticed or would not be sufficiently remedied. However, almost every speech difficulty is benefitted to no small degree by good choral speaking.

The day in the Rudolf Steiner School begins with speech exercises or poems recited in unison, for speaking awakens the one who speaks. Listening tends to make us sleepy. After concentrating on a long lesson, the class can be brought fresh and alive again by standing up and reciting a poem.

All this, however, is not so easy as it sounds. One boy yawns out loud and another collapses against his desk, a little girl fiddles with her neighbor's skirt. It takes experience, imagination and vitality to get the children to stand up straight and speak out with strength, clarity and enthusiasm. Once they come into the full swing of the recitation, color begins to rise in their cheeks and their eyes brighten. The teacher has attained her goal. Or, let us say, she has passed Scylla. Now she must beware her Charybdis; for once stimulated by this exciting element, the boys and girls—like wild horses—are apt to take the bits into their teeth and tear off into a chaos of galloping sound. To prevent disaster, the newly unleashed energy must immediately be guided into the exacting demands of sharply-formed consonants, of a particular phrasing of thought, of a deliberate change of rhythm. In concluding the recitation the teacher must bring it over into a self-contained quiet so that the children sit down again not only awakened but self-possessed and concentrated.

The poems which they learn are usually chosen because they express a highlight or epitomize the mood or content of their main lesson work. The teacher speaks to the class, before presenting the poem, in such a way as to develop an understanding for its thoughts and to create an atmosphere out of which it is to be spoken. She, of course, knows it by heart and has already worked out most of the changes and phrasing implicit in its form before she speaks it for them. They learn it entirely by ear. Only the older children sometimes learn poems cold from the printed page. Each day the class works together on one or another element in the poem. One day the rhythm is stressed, another day the dynamic motion of certain lines or the quality of the consonants that color a verse. Gradually the poem emerges into greater fullness, contrasts and clarity. When it is finally recited in an assembly the teacher, alas, is almost always disappointed. The children have been sitting quietly for a long time; they are anxious to "be good" and she misses something of the joy, vitality and spontaneity which rang out when they were alone together in the classroom.

Speech chorus is actually a highly economic means of teaching, for through it, in a short time, a teacher can refresh, enliven and train each child in a large group and bring to each one simultaneously a variety of valuable experiences.

The pictures in a poem fill a child's imagination; through them his sympathy for the world and his enthusiasm for beauty are awakened. His ear learns to follow the melody of the vowels and the sculpture of the consonants. He breathes deep with the wonderful surge, swing, skip and ripple of the rhythm. And these things he learns to appreciate not just with an aesthetic passivity but with active artistry. As the poem moves from enthusiasm to defeat, from bitterness to joy, his whole inward being becomes more agile, pliable and lively. The boys soon learn that this is no idle "playing around," but that often every bit of their strength is not enough to fulfill the demands of a powerful passage, and that they must be every bit as active and skillful as on the baseball field if they are to cut the consonants sharply enough and throw them home in just the right dramatic slice or curve.

They learn, too, that art is practice and has definite laws of clarity, rhythm, phrasing and gesture. They learn that the speaking of a poem is new each time and each time requires new effort and new awareness. So they become a little less apt to expect life to be "easy," to expect things to turn out "right" at the first try, a little less apt to despair when efforts fail and to become interested not only in the final result but in the *processes* of achievement as well. Like the violinist they learn the difficulty and delight of disciplined tempo change and of dramatic crescendo that mounts like a wave, mounts, waits, and then—just at the right moment—breaks with full decisive force.

As the children work over and over again to form the consonants exactly and livingly, they grow more alert. As they speak with fuller power and carry a long thought through on one long breath, the diaphragm grows stronger and the circulation stirs. Indeed good, vigorous recitation constitutes one of the best possible physical "breathing exercises," for it requires a natural deep breathing which strengthens the diaphragm muscles. When the children speak out fully in reciting a poem, not only do their lungs grow strong through exercise and fill with freshness, but the soul, too, "breathes," so to speak, expanding in wonder and courage, contracting in concentrated thought or earnestness; and the "in-spired", ideal element of the poem acts as a kind of inner oxygen that quickens their thoughts with life and eagerness.

In this way they learn a good many poems by heart and these become a part of themselves. Because of them they look at the world with new eyes, with new sympathy and appreciation. Poems learned early in life mean something to us in a way that no other poems quite can. They belong to us and rise up in us at odd or at critical moments to comfort or to help us see the world in its full color and subtlety.

It is true that a poem recited in chorus may often seem monotonous, but if you listen carefully you will be able to hear that the children are learning certain basic laws of phrasing, of projecting the voice and are gaining a sense of dramatic direction quickly and intelligently.

There is still another important aspect of choral speaking. Under cover of the sound of the many voices, the timid children forget themselves or summon up the courage to speak out as they never would otherwise; the leaders take pride in helping carry the weaker voices, but as soon as they become over-ambitious or show off, it becomes quite objectively obvious that they "stick out" and spoil the chorus. Each child depends upon and must adapt himself to the others, and this educates him to be an active, adaptable part of a social entity.

This is one of the times when a class is active as a whole. They all work together on shaping one and the same creation. They feel, at least at moments, the warmth, joy and thrill of this selfless companionship and are united by a common, ideal goal to which each one contributes his particular individual note. As a teacher works in this way with a group of children and experiences the concentrated, musical, sometimes lofty mood that is brought about in a classroom, she may well be reminded of how effective an instrument the ancient Greek chorus became in the days when the theater was a great educative force in the world.

(1973)   Christy Barnes

Acknowledgments

As former editor of "Education as an Art," following Christy Barnes, my thanks went many years ago to the busy teachers who sent in the articles you find in this volume, written in time snatched on weekends, on holidays, or when the evening preparation had been done.

This year again they responded cheerfully to my request for birth dates and life descriptions. Is it not an inspiring list of courageous pioneers? What pictures flash into our minds when we read "taught 37 years in the New York school" or "founded the first school in the State of . . ."! Take note of the many who have entered the spiritual world and may still be guiding stars to "their children".

Thanks to those who helped so cheerfully, too, to put these two volumes together: Gerald Karnow, M.D., editor and publisher, David Alsop, Eleanor Chandler, Lisl Francescelli, Marcie Winston, Maryann Perlman, Walter Teutsch. And special thanks to all those English, Dutch, German, Swiss, and American children who brought their bright eyes and enthusiastic hearts to the teachers they loved.

Ruth Pusch

Biographies

TRUDE AMANN ("Color in Childhood")
Pioneer in the Camphill Movement. Followed Karl König from Vienna to help establish the first community for the handicapped in Aberdeen, Scotland, where she taught.

CHRISTY BARNES ("Choral Recitation")
(b. 1909) Class teacher and then high school English teacher at the Rudolf Steiner School, N.Y.C.; created, directed the literary magazine there. Speech artist, speech teacher, poet, lecturer. Editor and manager of Adonis Press. Former editor of "Education as an Art" and "Journal for Anthroposophy".

HENRY BARNES ("Independent Schools and Independent Teachers"/"Some Characteristics of Steiner Education")
(b. 1912) For 35 years class teacher, history teacher and chairman of the faculty at the Rudolf Steiner School, N.Y.C. Cofounder of the Rudolf Steiner Educational and Farming Association, Harlemville, N.Y. Advisor for many Waldorf schools. General Secretary of the Anthroposophical Society in America. Lecturer and author.

HELEN BELSTERLI (Translated "On the Moral Education of Young Children")
An early member of the Threefold Group of the Anthroposophical Society, NYC, she translated many articles for their publications and spent her last years at the Threefold Farm, Spring Valley NY.

SUSANNE BERLIN ("In Third Grade")
(b. 1923) Attended the original Waldorf school in Stuttgart, where she later received her teacher training. Taught in private schools in Mexico before becoming a class teacher at the Waldorf School of Garden City. There for 33 years, she graduated five eighth grades. Now a visiting advisor to several Waldorf schools.

VIRGINIA FIELD BIRDSALL ("First Lessons in Botany")
(1878-1964) With Irene Foltz founded in 1928 the first Waldorf school in the United States, the Rudolf Steiner School in New York. Was class teacher and faculty chairman until 1941 when, with Elisabeth Grunelius, the second school was founded, Kimberton Farms, in Pennsylvania. Here she served as class

teacher, faculty chairman and school librarian until retirement in 1957.

CHRISTOPH BOY ("On the Moral Education of Young Children")

(1887-1934) Called to the first Waldorf school in Stuttgart, Germany by Rudolf Steiner in 1921. He remained a class teacher there until his death. In the difficult years before World War II he took on the responsibilities of administrator for the school and fought unremittingly for its continuation. As a teacher he had made the questions of moral life and moral education his particular task.

MARGARETHE BUEHLER ("Eurythmy Lessons for Children from Three to Seven")

(b. 1911) Widow of the Swiss-German poet Paul Buehler. Has taught children's eurythmy for many years in Dornach, Switzerland, and elsewhere.

FRANCIS EDMUNDS ("Feeling in the Growing Child")

(1902-1989) Taught for many years and served as faculty chairman at Michael Hall, England; teacher and advisor at Waldorf schools around the world. Lectured and started things in various countries. Founder and principal of Emerson College, Forest Row, Sussex, until his death. Author of *Rudolf Steiner's Gift to Education* and *Anthroposophy as a Healing Force*.

JOHN F. GARDNER ("Pressure and the Spirit of Play")

(b. 1912) With his wife Carol taught 1935-1937 at the Rudolf Steiner School, N.Y. Was called by Adelphi University in the late '40s to supervise development of its fledgling Waldorf School in Garden City, N.Y. There he remained for 30 years, serving as faculty chairman for 25 of them. Founder and director of Adelphi's Waldorf Institute for Liberal Education. Author of *The Experience of Knowledge* (1975) and *Heralds of the American Spirit* (1991).

MARTHA HAEBLER ("The Perfection of the Human Hand Lies in its Imperfection")

(1896-1966) Called to the original Waldorf school in Stuttgart in 1923 by Rudolf Steiner as class teacher, she carried two classes through eighth grade before the school was closed by the Nazis in 1938. After the war she returned to the school as class teacher, later as language teacher.

GLADYS HAHN (Translator of many articles)

(b. 1897) Taught kindergarten in the early years of the Rudolf Steiner School NYC. Curative eurythmist, teacher and director in the first work in America for the mentally handicapped preceding the Camphill Movement. Taught school classes for staff children at Camphill Village NY, the nucleus for what later became Hawthorne Valley School in Harlemville NY.

WILLIAM HARRER ("What Do We Mean by Education as an Art?"/"Man and Animal"/"Multiplication Tables Can Be Interesting")

(1905-1978) Born in southern Germany, had his Waldorf teacher training in Stuttgart, taught briefly in England at Kings Langley. He served the rest of his active life, 34 years, at the Rudolf Steiner School, N.Y.C. as class teacher and administrator. He and his wife Dorothy founded and directed Camp Glenbrook in New Hampshire.

FREDERICK HIEBEL ("The Importance of Fairy Tales in a Rudolf Steiner School")

(1903-1989) Poet, dramatist, biographer, essayist; came from his native Vienna in the early '30s to the U.S. Taught in the Rudolf Steiner School, N.Y.C., Wagner College, Rutgers and Princeton. His field was German literature; he published important studies of Goethe and Novalis. Became in 1963 a member of the Vorstand of the General Anthroposophical Society in Dornach, Switzerland; edited the weekly, *Das Goetheanum;* author of *The Gospel of Hellas, Shakespeare and The Awakening of Modern Consciousness, Time of Decision with Rudolf Steiner,* and many others.

ALAN HOWARD ("Activity in Education")

(b. 1907) Born and brought up in Bristol, England. Began teaching in 1930; served in the British army during World War II. On returning home he found his children attending the Waldorf school in Ilkeston and he soon became a class teacher there, also several times Faculty Chairman. Edited "Child and Man," the magazine for Waldorf Education in Great Britain, before it combined with "Education as an Art" in 1982. Contributed to the Educational Supplement of the London Times. Emigrated to Canada in 1968 and became a founding member and class teacher of the Toronto Waldorf School. Retired in 1972, moved to Vancouver, B.C., lectured on education, anthroposophy, became co-editor of "Education as an Art" up to its final number. His books include *You Wanted to Know What a Waldorf School Is and What it is Not; Nativity Stories; Thinking About Thinking; Sex in the Light of Reincarnation and Freedom.*

IRMGARD HUERSCH ("The Role of the Class Teacher and its Transformation")
(b. 1924) Born in Switzerland. Has been teaching since 1952 at the Rudolf Steiner School in Hamburg-Nienstedten, Germany, first as class teacher, then literature and history in the upper school as well as the free religion sessions.

EILEEN HUTCHENS ("The Teaching of Writing")
(1902-1987) Taught at the Leeds, England, High School in the '20s; worked at Sunfield Children's Home. Founder-teacher at Elmfield Steiner School at Stourbridge. Taught in both lower and upper school; teacher training. Writer, lecturer, storyteller, co-editor of "Child and Man."

ALICE SMITH JANSEN ("The Kindergarten in the Rudolf Steiner School")
(1899-1982) Followed Margaret Peckham and Gladys Barnett (Hahn) in the kindergarten of the Rudolf Steiner School, N.Y.C., serving until the end of the '30s.

BETTY KANE (STALEY), FRANKLIN KANE ("Earth, Who Gives to Us...")
Class teachers at Sacramento Waldorf School. Betty (b. 1938) helped start the high school and has been teaching literature, history, and history of art there for 16 years. Active in teacher-training at Rudolf Steiner College, Sacramento. Has lectured and given workshops on Waldorf education and parenting for the past 20 years.

RUDOLF KISCHNICK ("Children's Play")
(1911-1963) Student of Count von Bothmer, first gymnastics teacher at the original Waldorf School in Stuttgart, Germany. Taught gymnastics at the schools in Berlin, Hanover, Hamburg, and Ulm. Was also class teacher. His book *Games, Gymnastics, Sports* is used and treasured in many Waldorf schools.

ELISABETH KLEIN ("Modelling as the Expression of the Child's Inner Being")
(1901-1983) Helped to found the first Waldorf school in Dresden in 1929; when it was forced to close in 1941 she wrote books for children and young people, as well as material for use in the

schools. Class teacher at the Hanover Waldorf School 1950-1965, taught also science in the upper school.

LONA KOCH ("Adventures in the Park")

(1902-1979) Born in Germany, trained in handcrafts, a sturdy "Wandervogel." Came to the United States in the '30s with husband and three sons who became students in the Rudolf Steiner School, N.Y.C. where Lona carried the pre-school/kindergarten for almost 20 years.

AL LANEY ("The First Waldorf School")

(1896-1988) Author of *Paris Herald: The Incredible Newspaper* and other books; for many years sports writer for the New York Herald Tribune. A parent and staunch supporter of the Rudolf Steiner School, N.Y.C.

PATRICIA LIVINGSTON ("Handwork in the Early Grades")

(b. 1924) Was a pupil at the Rudolf Steiner School, N.Y. soon after it began in 1928 and until 1935. Returned there in 1956 as handwork teacher. Remained for 26 years, serving in every area, especially teacher training. Is now consultant to all North American Waldorf schools and chairman of the Pedagogical Section Council.

RUTH McARDLE ("The Effect of Waldorf Education on Home Life")

In 1978 she had been for many years a parent of three students at Green Meadow Waldorf School, Spring Valley, N.Y.

GISELA O'NEIL ("Gratitude-Love-Responsibility"/"Work with Underprivileged Children")

(1924-1988) Class and mathematics teacher at Highland Hall School, Los Angeles; Rudolf Steiner School, N.Y.C.; Green Meadow Waldorf School, Spring Valley, N.Y. Leader of study groups on Waldorf education. Lecturer, writer, editor.

VIRGINIA PAULSEN ("A Teacher Talks to Her Children")

(b. 1918) Her first grade was at Kimberton Farms School. Her next first grade, carried up to sixth, was at the Rudolf Steiner School, NYC. Then came three more first grades that Virginia took through to high school, followed by four years of high school English and many years as elementary and upper school librarian. She retired after 37 years at the Rudolf Steiner School.

MARGARET PECKHAM ("Beginning Bible Stories")

(1887-1966) The first American teacher to travel to Stuttgart, for a four-month training at the first Waldorf school (1926). Inaugurated the kindergarten in the New York school and shortly thereafter became a class teacher. Retired in the '50s.

RUTH PUSCH

(b. 1907) Taught eurythmy at the Rudolf Steiner School, NYC, Kimberton Farms School, High Mowing, kindergarten at the Garden City School, high school English at the New York school. Editor of the Rudolf Steiner School Association bulletin, "Education as an Art", which later became the organ of the Waldorf Schools of North America.

CHRISTIANE SORGE (Translated "Modelling as the Expression of the Child's Inner Being")

Language teacher , then class teacher at the Rudolf Steiner School, NYC in the '40s and '50s until her retirement.

MARJORIE SPOCK ("Too Much Like Work?")

(b. 1904) Has taught at the Dalton School, Ethical Culture School, Rudolf Steiner School, N.Y.C., and the Waldorf School of Garden City. Eurythmist, translator, author: *Teaching as a Lively Art; Eurythmy; Reflections on Community Building* and others. Biodynamic farmer in Maine.

BETTY STALEY, (Introduction) See Betty Kane

KARI VAN OORDT ("How Eurythmy Works in the Curriculum")

(b. 1908) Has taught eurythmy and performed the art in England, Norway, Switzerland, Yugoslavia, Mexico, and the United States. Eurythmy teacher at the Rudolf Steiner School, N.Y.C. for 21 years. One of the three founding directors of the Spring Valley Eurythmy School.

JAN VAN WETTUM ("Imagination at Different Ages")

(1900-1989) Teacher at the Vrije (Waldorf) School in the Hague, Holland as class teacher, then math and physics in the upper school; was also a free religion teacher there. Active in South African Waldorf schools 1969-1988.

CLARA VON WOEDTKE (Translated "The Perfection of the Human Hand")

A registered nurse and curative teacher in Switzerland at the Sonnenhof, Arlesheim, and then at Lossing School, Dover Plains, NY.

WILHELM ZUR LINDEN ("The Inner Being of Children's Diseases: Measles")

(1896-1972) Dr. zur Linden practiced in Berlin as a specialist in pediatrics. During World War II he was in charge of a large military hospital in Czechoslovakia. Condemned to death for his antagonism to the Nazi cause, he was rescued, taken prisoner, but soon released by the U.S. Army. In 1945 he opened a practice in Bad Godesberg where he worked until his death as pediatrician, particularly successful in developing a polio treatment from indications of Rudolf Steiner. In 1966 he published his autobiography *Blick durch's Prisma*. His article was taken from a later book whose first part has been translated and published in English as *A Child is Born* (Rudolf Steiner Press, London 1973).

BOOKS ON WALDORF EDUCATION

By Rudolf Steiner

The Child's Changing Consciousness
The Education of the Child in the Light of Anthroposophy
The Four Temperaments
Education as a Social Problem
Education and Modern Spiritual Life
Human Values in Education
An Introduction to Waldorf Education
The Roots of Education
The Renewal of Education
Soul Economy and Waldorf Education
Deeper Insights into Education
Self-Education: Autobiographical Reflections
Balance in Teaching
Study of Man
Practical Advice for Teachers
Discussions with Teachers
Waldorf Education for Adolescence
The Kingdom of Childhood

By other authors

Aeppli, Willi: *Rudolf Steiner Education and the Developing Child*
A.W.S.N.A.: *Multiculturalism in Waldorf Education*
Baldwin, Rahima: *You Are Your Child's First Teacher*
Barnes, H..,Howard, A.,Davy, J.: *An Introduction to Waldorf Education*
Benians, John: *The Golden Years*
Britz-Crecelius, Heidi: *Children at Play: Preparation for Life*
Carlgren, Frans: *Education Towards Freedom*
Edmunds, Francis: *Rudolf Steiner Education*
Edmunds, Francis: *Renewing Education*
Gabert, Erich: *Educating the Adolescent: Discipline or Freedom*
Gardner, John F.: *The Experience of Knowledge*
Grunelius, Elisabeth: *Early Childhood Education*
Haller, Ingeborg: *How Children Play*

Harwood, A.C.: *The Recovery of Man in Childhood*
The Way of a Child
Koepke, Hermann: *On the Threshold of Adolescence*
Encountering the Self: Transformation and Destiny in the Ninth Year
Lievegoed, Bernard: *Phases of Childhood*
Mitchell, D./Masters, B.: *Rudolf Steiner Waldorf Education*
Piening, E./Lyons, N.: *Educating as an Art*
Querido, René: *Creativity in Education*
Richards, M.C.: *Toward Wholeness: Rudolf Steiner Education in America*
Schwartz, Eugene: *Rhythms and Turning Points in the Life of the Child*
Setzer, Valdemar: *Computers in Education*
Sleigh, Julian : *Thirteen to Nineteen: Discovering the Light*
Spock, Marjorie: *Teaching as a Lively Art*
Staley, Betty: *Between Form and Freedom*
Wilkinson, Roy: *Commonsense Schooling*
von Heydebrand, Caroline: *Childhood: A Study of the Growing Child*
The Curriculum of the First Waldorf School

This is a short selection of books on Waldorf Education available at the Anthroposophic Press:

Bells Pond Star Route
Hudson, NY 12534

and

Rudolf Steiner College Book Service
9200 Fair Oaks Blvd.
Fair Oaks, CA 95628

Ask for catalogs, also at:

Mercury Press
241 Hungry Hollow Road
Spring Valley, NY 10977

Inquire at the Rudolf Steiner Library

RD#2 Harlemville
Ghent, NY 12075

concerning their services.

"Child and Man", a Journal for Rudolf Steiner Waldorf Education (2 copies per year), Subscriptions $9.60.

At The Sprig, Ashdown Road, Forest Row,
East Sussex RH 18 5 HP, England

202

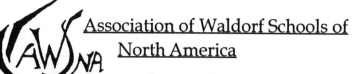

Association of Waldorf Schools of North America

David Alsop, Chairman
3911 Bannister Road
Fair Oaks, CA 95628
(916) 961-0927

The Association is a not-for-profit organization whose purpose it is to support and encourage the work of all Waldorf schools in North America.

"Renewal: A Journal for Waldorf Education" is published twice a year for individual members and for affiliated schools of the Association of Waldorf Schools of North America. Individual membership is $30.

Waldorf Schools in North America – 1993

CALIFORNIA:

Rudolf Steiner College, 9200 Fair Oaks Blvd.,
Fair Oaks, CA., 95628, 916-961-8727

Waldorf Institute of Southern California, 17100 Superior Street,
Northridge, CA., 91325, 818-349-1394

Pasadena Waldorf School, 209 E. Mariposa St.,
Altadena, CA., 91001-5133, 818-794-9564

Live Oak Waldorf School, P.O. Box 57,
Applegate, CA., 95703, 916-878-8720

Waldorf School of Mendocino County, 6280 Third Street P.O. Box 349,
Calpella, CA., 95418, 707-485-8719

Waldorf School Of Monterey, P.O. Box 221057,
Carmel, CA., 93922, 408-372-4677

Mariposa Waldorf School, P.O. Box 1210,
Cedar Ridge, CA., 95924, 916-272-8411

Davis Waldorf School, 3100 Sycamore Lane,
Davis, CA, 95616, 916-753-1651

East Bay Waldorf School, 1275 61st Street,
Emeryville, CA., 94608, 415-547-1842

Sacramento Waldorf School, 3750 Bannister Road,
Fair Oaks, CA., 95628, 916-961-3900

Waldorf Community School, 11792 Bushard Street,
Fountain Valley, CA, 92708, 714-963-3637

Sierra Waldorf School, 19234 Rawhide Road,
Jamestown, CA, 95327, 209-984-0454

Waldorf School of the Peninsula, 401 Rosita Avenue,
Los Altos, CA., 94022, 415-948-8433

Highland Hall School, 17100 Superior Street,
Northridge, CA., 91325, 818-349-1394

Cedar Springs Waldorf School, 6029 Gold Meadows Road,
Placerville, CA, 95667, 916-642-9903

Camellia Waldorf School, 5701 Freeport Blvd.,
Sacramento, CA, 95822, 916-427-5022

San Francisco Waldorf School, 2938 Washington St.,
San Francisco, CA., 94115, 415-931-2750

Marin Waldorf School, 755 Idylberry Dr.,
San Rafael, CA., 94903, 415-479-8190

Waldorf School of Santa Barbara, 2300 B Garden Street,
Santa Barbara, CA., 93105, 805-569-2558

Santa Cruz Waldorf School, 2190 Empire Grade,
Santa Cruz, CA., 95060, 408-425-0519

Santa Monica Waldorf School, 1512 Pearl Street,
Santa Monica, CA, 90405, 213-450-0349

Summerfield Waldorf School, 155 Willowside Ave.,
Santa Rosa, CA., 95401, 707-575-7194

Sonoma Valley Waldorf School, Box 2063,
Sonoma, CA, 95476, 707-996-0996

Waldorf School of San Diego, 3327 Kenora Drive,
Spring Valley, CA., 91977, 619-589-6404

COLORADO:

Aspen Waldorf School, PO Box 1563, Aspen, CO, 81612, 303-925-7938

Shining Mountain School, 987 Locust,
Boulder, CO., 80304, 303-444-7697

Denver Waldorf School, 735 East Florida,
Denver, CO., 80210, 303-777-0531

FLORIDA:

Gainesville Waldorf School, 921 SW Depot Ave.,
Gainesville, FL., 32601, 904-375-6291

GEORGIA:

The Children's Garden, 2089 Ponce de Leon Avenue,
Atlanta, GA, 30307, 404-371-9470

HAWAII:

Haleakala School, R.R. 2, Box 790, Kula, Maui, HI., 96790, 808-878-2511

Honolulu Waldorf School, 350 Ulua Street,
Honolulu, HI., 96821, 808-377-5471

Kauai Waldorf School, PO Box 818, Kilauea, HI, 96754, 808-828-1144

Malamalama School, SR 13031, Keaau, HI., 96749, 808-966-9901

Pali Uli School, Box 1338, Kealakekua, HI, 96750, 808-322-3316

ILLINOIS:

Chicago Waldorf School, 1651 West Diversey,
Chicago, IL., 60614, 312-327-0079

MAINE:

Ashwood School, RR 1, Box 4725,
  Lincolnville, ME., 04849, 207-236-8021

Merriconeag School, P.O. Box 336,
  So. Freeport, ME., 04078, 207-865-3900

MARYLAND:

Waldorf School Of Baltimore, 4701 Yellowwood Ave.,
  Baltimore, MD., 21209, 301-367-6808

Washington Waldorf School, 4800 Sangamore Road,
  Bethesda, MD., 20816, 301-229-6107

MASSACHUSETTS:

Cape Ann School, 668 Hale Street,
  Beverly Farms, MA., 01915, 508-927-8811

Beach Rose Waldorf School, 85 Cotuit Road,
  Bourne, MA., 02532-0912, 508-563-9016

Rudolf Steiner School of G. B., West Plain Road,R.D.1, Box37B,
  Great Barrington, MA., 01230, 413-528-4015

The Hartsbrook Waldorf School, 94 Bay Road,
  Hadley, MA., 01035, 413-586-1908

The Lexington Waldorf School, 739 Massachusetts Avenue,
  Lexington, MA., 02173, 617-863-1062

MICHIGAN:

Rudolf Steiner School of Ann Arbor, 2775 Newport Road,
  Ann Arbor, MI., 48103, 313-995-4141

Oakland Steiner School, 1050 East Square Lake Road,
  Bloomfield Hills, MI, 48304, 313-646-2540

Detroit Waldorf School, 2555 Burns Ave.,
  Detroit, MI., 48214, 313-822-0300

MINNESOTA:

City of Lakes Waldorf School, 3450 Irving Ave. South,
  Minneapolis, MN, 55408, 612-822-1092

Minnesota Waldorf School, 2129 Fairview Ave. North,
  Roseville, MN., 55113-5416, 612-636-6577

NEW HAMPSHIRE:

Monadnock Waldorf School, 98 South Lincoln Street,
  Keene, NH., 03431, 603-357-4442

Antioch Waldorf Teacher Training Program, Roxbury Street,
Keene, NH., 03431, 603-357-3122

High Mowing School, Wilton, NH., 03086, 603-654-2391

Pine Hill Waldorf School, Wilton, NH., 03086, 603-654-6003

NEW JERSEY:

Waldorf School Of Princeton, 1062 Cherry Hill Rd. RD#3,
Princeton, NJ., 08540, 609-466-1970

NEW MEXICO:

Santa Fe Waldorf School, Rt. 9, Box 50-B3,
Santa Fe, NM., 87505, 505-983-9727

NEW YORK:

Waldorf Institute of Sunbridge College, 260 Hungry Hollow Road,
Spring Valley, NY., 10977, 914-425-0055

Rudolf Steiner School, 15 East 79th Street,
New York, NY., 10021, 212-535-2130

Green Meadow Waldorf School, Hungry Hollow Road,
Spring Valley, NY., 10977, 914-356-2514

Waldorf School of Garden City, Cambridge Avenue,
Garden City, NY., 11530, 516-742-3434

Hawthorne Valley School, R.D. 2, Harlemville,
Ghent, NY., 12075, 518-672-7092

Waldorf School of the Finger Lakes, 855 Five Mile Drive,
Ithaca, NY., 14850, 607-273-4088

Mountain Laurel Waldorf School, 304 Rt. 32N,
New Paltz, NY., 12561, 914-255-9225

Spring Hill School, 62-66 York Ave,
Saratoga Springs, NY., 12866, 518-584-7643

Aurora Waldorf School, 525 West Falls Road,
West Falls, NY, 14170, 716-655-2029

NORTH CAROLINA:

Emerson Waldorf School, 6211 New Jericho Road,
Chapel Hill, NC., 27516, 919-967-1858

OHIO:

Spring Garden School, 2141 Pickle Road,
Akron, OH., 44312, 216-644-1160

Cincinnati Waldorf School, 5411 Moeller Ave,
Norwood, OH., 45212, 513-531-5135

OREGON:

The Waldorf School, P.O. Box 3240,
  Ashland, OR., 97520, 503-482-9825

Eugene Waldorf School, 1350 McLean Blvd.,
  Eugene, OR., 97405, 503-683-6951

Portland Waldorf School, 109 NE 50th Ave.,
  Portland, OR., 97213-2907, 503-245-1507

PENNSYLVANIA:

Kimberton Waldorf School, West Seven Star Road,
  Kimberton, PA., 19442, 215-933-3635

Susquehanna Waldorf School, 15 West Walnut Street,
  Marietta, PA, 17547, 717-426-4506

RHODE ISLAND:

Meadowbrook Waldorf School, P.O. Box 508,
  W. Kingston, RI., 02892, 401-782-1312

TEXAS:

Austin Waldorf School, 8702 South View Road,
  Austin, TX., 78737, 512-288-5942

VERMONT:

Lake Champlain Waldorf School, 27 Harbor Road,
  Shelburne, VT., 05482, 802-985-2827

Green Mountain School, RR 1 Box 4885,
  Wolcott, VT., 05680, 802-888-2828

VIRGINIA:

Crossroads Waldorf School, Route 3, Box 189,
  Crozet, VA., 22932, 804-823-6800

WASHINGTON:

Whatcom Hills Waldorf School, 941 Austin Street,
  Bellingham, WA., 98226, 206-733-3164

Whidbey Island Waldorf School, Box 469,
  Clinton, WA., 98236, 206-321-5686

Olympia Waldorf School, P.O. Box 638,
  East Olympia, WA, 98540, 206-493-0906

Seattle Waldorf School, 2728 N.E. 100th,
  Seattle, WA., 98125, 206-524-5320

WISCONSIN:

Waldorf School of Milwaukee, 718 East Pleasant Street,
Milwaukee, WI., 53202, 414-272-7727

Prairie Hill Waldorf School, N14 W29143 Silvernail Road,
Pewaukee, WI, 53072, 414-691-8996

Pleasant Ridge Waldorf School, 321 East Decker,
Viroqua, WI., 54665, 608-637-7828

CANADA:

Rudolf Steiner Centre, PO Box 18,
Thornhill, Ontario, L3T 3N1, 416-764-7570, Adults

Calgary Waldorf School, 1915 36th Ave. S.W.,
Calgary, ALBERTA, T2T 2G6, 403-287-1868

Halton Waldorf School, 83 Campbellville Road E.,
Campbellville, ONTARIO, L0P 1B0, 416-854-0191

Aurora Rudolf Steiner School, 7211 - 96 A Avenue,
Edmonton, ALBERTA, T6B 1B5, 403-469-2101

Sunrise Waldorf School, 4344 Peters Road,
Duncan, B.C., V9L 4W4, 604-743-7253

London Waldorf School, 1697 Trafalgar Square,
London, ONTARIO, N5W 1X2, 519-451-7971

Nelson Waldorf School, Box 165,
Nelson, B.C., V1L 5P9, 604-352-6919

Ottawa Waldorf School, 10 Coral Avenue,
Nepean, ONTARIO, K2E 5Z6, 613-226-7369

Vancouver Waldorf School, 2725 St. Christopher's Road,
N. Vancouver, B.C., V7K 2B6, 604-985-7435

L'Ecole Rudolf Steiner de Montreal, 12050 Bois de Boulogne,
Montreal, QUEBEC, H3M 2X9, 514-334-5291

Toronto Waldorf School, Box 220, 9100 Bathurst st.,
Thornhill, ONTARIO, L3T 3N3, 416-881-1611

Kelowna Waldorf School, Box 93, 429 Collett Road,
Okanaga Mission, B.C., V0H 1S0, 604-764-4130

Alan Howard Waldorf School, 228 St. George Street,
Toronto, ONTARIO, M5R 2N9, 416-975-1349

MEXICO:

Colegio Waldorf de Cuernavaca, Jesus H. Preciado 103
Col. San Anton, Cuernavaca, Morelos, Mexico, 7318-8576

Rudolf Steiner/Waldorf Schools World List
(as of February 1993)

ARGENTINA: Buenos Aires (2)

AUSTRALIA: Adelaide, Bangalow, Bowral, Cawongla, Dorrigo, Hazelbrook, Maitland, Melbourne (3), Mount Barker, Nedlands, Newcastle, Perth, Sydney (3), Thora, Victoria/Yarro, Weston Creek, Yarramundi.

AUSTRIA: Graz, Innsbruck, Klagenfurt, Salzburg, Vienna (3).

BELGIUM: Aalst, Affligem, Antwerp (4), Brasschaat, Brugge (2), Brussels, Eupen, Gent, Leuven, Lier, Overijse, Raeren, Spa, Turnhout, Wilrijt.

BRAZIL: Botucatu, Camanducaia, Florianopolis, Riberao Preto, Sao Paulo (3).

CZECH REPUBLIC: Prague

CHILE: Santiago (2)

COLOMBIA: Cali, Medellin.

DENMARK: Aalborg, Åarhus (2), Copenhagen (2), Esbjerg, Fredericia, Hjørring, Kvistgård, Merløse, Odense (2), Risskov, Silkeborg, Skanderborg, Vejle, Vordingborg.

ECUADOR: Quito (2)

EGYPT: Bilbeis

ESTONIA: Polvamaa, Rakvere, Tallinn, Tartu

FINLAND: Espoo, Helsinki (2), Jyväskylä, Kuopio, Lahti, Lappeenranta, Oulu, Pori, Rovaniemi, Sammatti, Seinäjoki, Tammisaari, Tampere, Turku, Vaasa, Vantaa.

FRANCE: Chatou (Paris), Colmar, Laboissiere, St. Faust de Haut (Pau), Saint Genis Laval, Saint-Menoux, Strasbourg (2), Troyes, Verrieres le Buisson.

GERMANY: Aachen, Augsburg, Bad Nauheim, Balingen, Benefeld, Bergisch Gladbach, Berlin (5), Bexbach, Bielefeld, Böblingen, Bochum, Bonn, Braunschweig, Bremen (2), Chemnitz, Chiemgau, Coburg,

Cologne, Cottbus, Darmstadt, Detmold, Dietzenbach, Dortmund (2), Dresden, Düsseldorf, Duisburg, Eckernförde, Elmshorn, Engelberg, Erftstadt-Liblar, Erlangen, Essen, Esslingen, Evinghausen, Filderstadt, Flensburg, Frankenthal, Frankfurt, Frankfurt/Oder, Freiburg (3), Friedrichstal, Gladbeck, Göppingen, Göttingen, Gütersloh, Haan-Gruiten, Hagen, Halle, Hamburg (7), Hamm, Hannover (2), Heidelberg, Heidenheim, Heilbronn, Hildesheim, Hof, Jena, Kakenstorf, Karlsruhe, Kassel, Kiel (4), Kleinmachnow, Krefeld, Leipzig, Lörrach, Loheland, Ludwigsburg, Lübeck, Lüneburg, Magdeburg, Mainz, Mannheim, Marburg, Minden, Mönchengladbach, Mülheim (2), Munich (4), Münster, Neumünster, Neuwied, Nuremberg, Nurtingen, Offenburg, Oldenburg, Otterberg, Ottersberg, Pforzheim, Potsdam, Remscheid, Rendsburg (2), Reutlingen, Saarbrücken, Schloss Hamborn, Schondorf, Schopfheim, Schwäbisch Gmünd, Schwäbish Hall, Siegen, Sindelfingen, Stade, St. Augustin, Stuttgart (3), Trier, Tübingen, Überlingen, Ulm (2), Vaihingen/Enz, Villingen-Schwenningen, Wahlwies, Wangen, Wanne-Eickel, Wattenscheid, Weimar, Werder, Wernstein, Wiehl, Wiesbaden, Witten (2), Wolfsburg, Würzburg, Wuppertal (2).

HOLLAND: Alkmaar (3), Almelo, Almere, Alphen, Amersfoort, Amstelveen, Amsterdam, Apeldoorn, Arnheim, Assen, Bergen (2), De Bilt, Den Bosch, Boxmeer, Breda (2), Brummen, Bussum, Delft, Deventer, Doetinchem, Dordrecht, Driebergen, Ede, Eindhoven (2), Emmen, Enschede, Gouda, s'Gravenhage (4), Groningen, The Hague, Den Helder, Haarlem (2), Harderwijk, Heerlen, Helmond, Hertogenbosch, Hillegom, Hilversum, Hoofddedorp, Hoorn, Krimpen/Ijssel, Leeuwarden, Leiden (3), Maastricht, Meppel, Middelburg (2), Nijmegen (3), Oldenzaal, Oosterhout, Oud Beijerland, Purmerend, Roermond, Roosendaal, Rotterdam (3) Sittard, Terneuzen, Den Burg Texel, Tiel, Tilberg, Uden, Utrecht, Venlo, Voorschoten, Wageningen, Winterswijk, Zaandam, Zeist (4), Zoetermeer, Zutphen (4), Zwolle.

HUNGARY: Budaörs, Budapest (2), Dunakeszi, Gödöllö, Györ, Solymar.

IRELAND: Cooleenbridge, Dublin

ISRAEL: Nazareth

ITALY: Albano, Bosentino, Meran, Milan, Oriago, Rome, Trieste.

JAPAN: Tokyo

KENYA: Nairobi

LIECHTENSTEIN: Schaan

LUXEMBOURG: Luxembourg

NEW ZEALAND: Auckland (2), Christchurch, Dunedin, Hastings, Tauranga, Wellington.

NORWAY: Alesund, As, Asker, Askim, Baerum, Bergen (2), Drammen, Fredrikstad, Gjovik/Toten, Haugesund, Hedemark, Hurum, Kristiansand, Lillehammer, Lorenskog, Moss, Nesoddtangen, Oslo (2), Ringerike, Stavanger, Tönsberg, Trondheim, Tromso.

PERU: Lima (2).

POLAND: Warsaw

PORTUGAL: Lagos

RUSSIA: Moscow, St. Petersburg

SLOVENIA: Ljubljana

SOUTH AFRICA: Alexandra, Cape Town (2), Durban, Johannesburg, Meadowlands, Natal, Pretoria.

SPAIN: Alicante, Madrid.

SWEDEN: Delsbo (2), Garpenberg, Göteborg, Höör, Järna (2), Kalmar, Kungälv, Linköping, Lund, Märsta, Norrköping, Nyköping, Örebro, Rörum, Stegehus, Söderköping, Stockholm (3), Täby, Umeå, Västerås.

SWITZERLAND: Aldiswil, Aesch, Arlesheim, Basel (4), Bern(2), Biel, Chur, Dornach, Geneva/Confignon, Glarisegg, Herisau, Ins, Kreuzlingen, Langenthal, Langnau, Lausanne, Lenzburg, Lugano, Lucerne, Marbach, Neuchâtel, Pratteln, Schaffhausen, Schuls-Tarasp, Solothurn, Spiez, St. Gallen, Wetzikon, Wil, Winterthur, Yverdun, Zug, Zurich (2).

UNITED KINGDOM: Aberdeen, Belfast, Botton, Brighton, Bristol, Canterbury, Dyfed, Edinburgh, Forest Row, Forres, Glasgow, Gloucester, Hereford, Ilkeston, Kings Langley, London (4), Oxford, Plymouth, Reading, Ringwood, St. Albans, Sheffield, Snowdonia, Stourbridge, Stroud (2), Totnes, Tunbridge Wells, York.

URUGUAY: Montevideo

Index